Praise for *A Witch's Ally*

"A far-reaching examination of the intersections between witchcraft, the inner world of animals, and our relationships with them. Throughout *A Witch's Ally*, you'll find a beautifully curated collection of Dodie's personal experiences, history, folklore, rituals, and frameworks to understand witchcraft with animals. I am especially appreciative of the care that is taken in clarifying the distinctions between pets, companions, animal spirits, and cultural contexts. This book is an asset to anyone that wishes to deepen their connection to the spiritual world of animals."

—**IVO DOMINGUEZ, JR.,** author of the Witch's Sun Sign series

"This profoundly wise and wonderful book is an extraordinary guide that opens the portals of the mind and spirit to the magical power of our connection with animals on both the physical and non-physical planes. Beautifully written, combining deep insight with practicality, *A Witch's Ally* is an important book that could change your perception of animals—and your life."

—**LISA TENZIN-DOLMA,** author of *The Glastonbury Tarot* and *Charlie, the Dog Who Came in from the Wild*

"McKay brings a modern, inclusive, and thorough lens to the discussion of animal companions to your craft. With its insights and techniques, this book will help you forge, deepen, and multiply your connections with the potential allies all around us, as well as inform you on the history and folklore behind many beyond the ubiquitous black cat and corvid."

—**J. R. MASCARO,** author of *Seal, Sigil & Call*

"*A Witch's Ally* thoughtfully presents the diverse roles animals have played in folklore throughout history and within modern witchcraft. The reader is immersed in the different relationships witches form with animals, exploring the origins of those bonds, and how the unique strengths of our companions can enhance magical practice. Adding a rich layer of insight to the narrative, *A Witch's Ally* goes beyond our perceptions of animals and considers how they perceive us and the world around them. This book is a beautifully written, heartfelt tribute to the animals that enrich our magic and our lives!"

—**NICOLETTE MIELE,** author of *Runes for the Green Witch*

"Our relationship with animals is pure magic, and Dodie taps into those feelings to help us re-enchant our relationship with our animal companions and indeed the role they can play in our own witchcraft practices. Animals, just like us, are imbued with spirit and soul, and *A Witch's Ally* offers a delectable slice of animism that so many of us can access, helping to see the world and all the beings in it as alive with spirit!"

—**EMMA KATHRYN,** author of *Season Songs* and *Witch Life*

A Witch's
ALLY

About the Author

Dodie Graham McKay is a writer, Green Witch, Gardnerian priestess, and filmmaker. She is inspired to document and share stories that capture the beauty of nature and the visible and invisible realms of magic and witchcraft. She is the author of the book *Earth Magic* (Llewellyn, 2021), and her documentary films include *The WinniPagans* (2012), *Starry Nights* (2016), and the four-part series *Exploring the Sacred* (2022). Dodie spends her spare time walking her dogs and facilitating a busy coven. She lives in Treaty One Territory, Homeland of the Red River Métis Nation, Winnipeg, Manitoba, Canada. Visit her at www.dodiegrahammckay.com.

A Witch's
ALLY

BUILDING A MAGICAL RELATIONSHIP WITH
ANIMAL FAMILIARS AND COMPANIONS

DODIE GRAHAM MCKAY

LLEWELLYN
WOODBURY, MINNESOTA

First Edition
First Printing, 2024

Book design by Christine Ha
Cover art and part page illustrations by Laura Tempest Zakroff
Cover design by Verlynda Pinckney

Llewellyn Publications is a registered trademark of Llewellyn Worldwide Ltd.

Library of Congress Cataloging-in-Publication Data (Pending)
ISBN: 978-0-7387-7011-6

Llewellyn Worldwide Ltd. does not participate in, endorse, or have any authority or responsibility concerning private business transactions between our authors and the public.

All mail addressed to the author is forwarded but the publisher cannot, unless specifically instructed by the author, give out an address or phone number.

Any internet references contained in this work are current at publication time, but the publisher cannot guarantee that a specific location will continue to be maintained. Please refer to the publisher's website for links to authors' websites and other sources.

Llewellyn Publications
A Division of Llewellyn Worldwide Ltd.
2143 Wooddale Drive
Woodbury, MN 55125-2989
www.llewellyn.com

Printed in the United States of America

Other Books by Dodie Graham McKay
Earth Magic

Forthcoming Books by Dodie Graham McKay
The Witch's Ally Oracle

For Oban, the Wonderdog
2001–2017
You are with me always
quietly padding along beside me from the world of spirit
gently sighing in the back seat of my car, forever
you are free of the collar, still hanging by the front door
your shade walks with me as it always has
and will
forevermore

Disclaimer

The publisher and author assume no liability for any injuries caused to the reader that may result from the reader's use of content contained in this publication and recommend common sense when contemplating the practices described in the work. In the following pages, you will find guidance for working with the remains of animals and recommendations for the use of certain essential oils, incense blends, and ritual items. If you are allergic to any items used in the workings, please refrain from use. Magical work is not meant to replace the care of a qualified medical professional.

Contents

Spells, Recipes & Workings

Foreword

"Seeming to prefer the companie of Beasts, they converse with them as equalls."[1] So says Edward Johnston, Esq., in his 1645 pamphlet describing the nature of witches. Upon delving into the annals of witchcraft history and folklore, it swiftly becomes evident how accurate Johnston was in his assertion. Witches and animals have perennially shared an inseparable bond, walking side by side along the crooked path—a relationship that continues to this day. Throughout history and in contemporary times, animals that share a connection with witches are bestowed with a distinctive title, one that underscores the equality alluded to by Johnston. Rather than being estranged from witches and viewed as separate or inferior, these animals are recognized as familiars.

The term *familiar* can be a complicated one as it has come to mean different things. If you ask a witch today whether they have a familiar, chances are they will point to their beloved pet. They will likely regale you with affectionate anecdotes about how their cat has a penchant for jumping on the altar during rituals or how their ferret helps pick tarot cards during readings. I grew up with such a mystical pet, a gray tabby cat named Moonbeam with whom I shared an intense telepathic connection. She was magic embodied in feline form, a guide, a healer, and a fierce protector. It was she who taught me some of the most important magical lessons, ones which I hold close to my heart. She was my familiar, and I was hers. Moonbeam passed away in 2017, her ashes mixed among the catnip and anise hyssop in the garden where we often played.

In contrast to Moonbeam and the modern conceptualization of familiars, the term did not originally refer to a physical pet but rather to the spirits with

---

1. Johnston, "Witche Ways," 26.

whom people consulted for various reasons, such as divining future events. The Bible contains several references to familiar spirits, including Leviticus 20:27, which states, "A man also or woman that hath a familiar spirit, or that is a wizard, shall surely be put to death: they shall stone them with stones: their blood shall be upon them."[2] The consultation of spirits was included in the later Witchcraft Acts of Great Britain. For example, the Witchcraft Act of 1604 included provisions against those who "consult, covenant with, entertaine, imploy, feed, or reward any evil and wicked spirit."[3]

By the time the Act of 1604 had been passed, the concept of familiar spirits had already become a central part of the witch trials—specifically in England and Scotland. Trial transcripts reveal that familiar spirits could materialize in a myriad of ways. For some they would take on a spectral humanoid form, such was the case for accused witches like Bessie Dunlop and Andro Man. More commonly, though, familiar spirits would appear in the shape of an animal. In describing familiar spirits, Puritan clergyman Richard Bernard explained how they may appear not only as a man, woman, or boy but also as "a browne and white Dogge, of a Foale, of a spotted Bitch, of a Hare, Moale, Cat, Kitling, Rat, dunne Chicken or Owle, of a Toade, or Crab."[4] Whichever form a familiar spirit might take, it was believed that they served witches as faithful factotums, assisting them in all kinds of magical endeavors for both good and ill.

During the witchcraft revival of the mid-twentieth century, many folkloric concepts, such as covens and sabbats, were being adapted for modern application. Despite this, it doesn't appear that familiars, in any form, were of much interest at the time. In a letter to Michael Howard, Cecil Williamson, the founder of the Museum of Witchcraft and Magic, recounts how he once tried to get Gerald Gardner interested in familiar spirits but to no avail.[5] It wasn't until 1970 that the topic of familiars was to be addressed in a book on modern witchcraft. The book in question, Paul Huson's *Mastering Witchcraft*, discusses three different types of familiars. The first is a totem animal, which symbolizes a coven's power. The second is a pet companion who aids a witch in spellwork.

---

2. "Leviticus 20:27–King James Version."
3. "1604: 1 James 1 c.12."
4. Bernard, *A Guide to Grand-Jury Men*, 41.
5. Patterson, *Cecil Williamson's Book of Witchcraft*, 178.

The third is a spirit who acts as both a magical servant and protector.[6] It was Huson's second type of a familiar, that of a magically inclined pet, that would eventually gain popularity amongst practitioners and become the definition commonly used.

That being said, in the last decade or so, as interest in folklore has had a resurgence among witches, there has been an increase in practitioners discussing familiars in the classical sense, that is to say as spirits. As per folklore, these spirits may appear in human form but tend to manifest as animals. While there has been some contention among practitioners regarding what defines a proper familiar, I believe there is room for a multifaceted definition that includes both spiritual and physical variations. I've been lucky enough to experience both forms in my life. In addition to the wise Moonbeam—and currently a handsome gerbil named Tom—I've come to work with a cunning familiar spirit who variously appears as a gallant man and a lively stag. It was in this latter form that I first encountered him in the woods one day many years ago.

All in all, what captivates me most is not the corporeality of familiars but rather the enduring inclination for them to manifest in the form of animals. Why is this? And why are witches, past and present, so partial to beasties both wild and domestic? Combining aspects of witchcraft, folklore, and natural science, the following book helps answer these questions and much more. Herein, Dodie offers not only her profound insight on the subject but also a heartfelt reminder that whether they be flesh and blood or ethereal, some of the most powerful allies we have as witches are those animals with whom we become most familiar.

—Kelden
December 2023

---

6. Huson, *Mastering Witchcraft*, 144–46.

Preface

On March 28, 2002, box turtles were all I could think of as I walked into the pet store. I just needed to pick up some food for Bert and Olive, my rescue box turtles. This particular store also served as a satellite adoption centre for the Humane Society. I could not resist poking my nose in to see the cats they had available. I already had four cats in addition to the two box turtles and a tank full of fish (more rescues). I had no interest in another pet, another mouth to feed, another responsibility. I also have allergies, and my menagerie caused me constant sinus congestion. So I just poked my nose in to see who was waiting for a new home. The kennels lined one wall, stacked three high with steel bars. Each kennel had a cat or two inside, and my heart broke as I walked along the cages. Little feline paws would reach out between the bars, looking for attention. I stooped down to peer into the last kennel, a slightly larger one than the rest. And that is when everything changed. Forever.

Looking back at me with the most intense and soulful brown eyes was a puppy. He was about six months old according to the tag on his cage, which also described the pup as a "male, bicolour, husky/terrier cross of unspecified origin." He had been found at a garbage dump in rural Manitoba. He had just arrived at the adoption centre earlier that day. We stared at each other for a long time. The first thing I remember saying out loud to him was "We belong together."

I spent that evening agonizing over the situation. I was allergic to pet fur, and I already had four cats! I went to see the pup the next day, and I was determined to spring him from the Humane Society and bring him home. So determined, in fact, that I had already secretly purchased a collar and leash and stashed them in the trunk of my car.

I arrived at the adoption centre and there he was, getting visited by a couple with a young child. My heart sank—they were going to scoop my puppy. I stood outside the adoption area, watching. The pup turned around and stared at me. I stared back. "I'm here to get you!" I said in my mind, as loud as I could think.

The family left and I moved in fast, explaining to the adoption coordinator that I was here for this dog. As I spoke to her, the dog—my dog—crouched and tried to poop. He was bleeding! The coordinator was shocked and quickly read his file—he had somehow been cleared for adoption without being seen by a veterinarian. He would have to stay at the adoption centre until he could earn a clean bill of health. It was Saturday, the next day was Easter Sunday, and the vet would not see him until regular business hours on Tuesday. Crushed, I left my name and number, and they promised they would call me if and when he was cleared to go home. I spent the next two days worried sick. He was my dog—my boy—and I was desperate for good news.

The call came to me at work on Tuesday afternoon. He was fine, just an upset tummy from eating trash at the garbage dump. After work I sped like a maniac to the Humane Society to pick up my dog. He was so happy to be out of there and seemed genuinely pleased to see me. His mood changed abruptly when we got to the parking lot. He was absolutely terrified of the car, so I had to pick him up and load him into the back seat. That night he was named Oban, a name chosen in honour of a memorable holiday in that seaside Scottish town. His first gesture in his new home was to walk up to my extremely grumpy cat, Cronos, and drop his only toy, a chewy bone, in front of the cat as if in offering. He won over the cat … eventually.

I was out of my comfort zone. I had no idea how to look after a dog. I had no idea that for the next fifteen and a half years, this dog would look after me.

Introduction

Witchcraft has a certain esthetic. Stacks of occult books, pointed hats, brooms, cauldrons, and various other implements. But no image could be more iconic than that of the witch with her black cat. We take for granted that this popular witch's companion will be a part of every story—the cunning familiar who can slink unseen through the shadows, informing her mistress of the goings-on in the village, gathering information, informing and advising the witch, and acting as a helper and companion. Maybe other creatures come to mind—a toad, an owl, or perhaps a snake. Why these animals? Why any animal?

A love of animals was instilled in me from a very young age. My mother was a single parent, and we always had a cat or three in our home. Then came the gerbils that my aunt rescued from her high school classroom at the end of term, then a guinea pig followed by a hamster, then a rat, named Grubby. I spent a lot of time at my grandparents' house, where Max and Charlie, the dogs, were my playmates. I was an only child, but I never lacked for companionship with the family menagerie around.

Into my teens I discovered witchcraft. This felt like a natural step for me and an opportunity to expand my love of the natural world into a viable and active spiritual practice. My mother had also raised me around radical and progressive political ideas and causes, and this also fit into the witchcraft I was attracted to. Environmentalism, animism, and magic wove in along with punk rock, social justice, art, and a love of reading. Diving ever deeper into magic, I found my way to Wicca. After a long and winding path, I initiated into the Gardnerian tradition and eventually became a high priestess. I now facilitate a busy coven as well as a book study group and a Pagan circle that meets regularly to celebrate the sabbats. Alongside my Gardnerian group activities, I also maintain a solitary practice that I describe as Deep Green Witchcraft. This is where my magic is influenced by the flora and fauna of the land I live on and a desire to find accord with the visible and invisible beings I share it with. My daily dog walks are a time to observe the changing of the seasons and the habits of the plentiful local wildlife that live in my neighbourhood. The area is surrounded on three sides by the looping Red River, and its banks form a wildlife corridor that is travelled by deer, beaver, racoons, foxes, muskrats, geese, ducks, and a cavalcade of migratory birds. I have come to realize that all of these creatures have a story to tell and a part to play in how magic moves in the world. But how to define it and how to describe it? I will try my best to get there in this book. The way a witch relates to animals in real modern life does not necessarily resemble our expectations based on the stories of the past.

Using this Book

An up-to-date discussion on the relationship between a witch and their animal familiar needs to have three elements—in my opinion, anyway. First, we need to look at our history and understand what is documented about witches and familiar beings to gain an understanding of where our expectations of magical relationships with the animal kingdom come from. Then, we need to take a pragmatic look at how we, as witches, relate to animals and endeavour to see the world from their unique points of view. Finally, we need to apply ourselves and integrate our knowledge into action.

Part 1 will go back in time and set the stage. Folklore abounds with tales of witches and their familiars—various beings that came from the spirit world and took many forms, not just those of animals. Some of the documents of magic and witchcraft speak of familiar spirits in the form of guardian angel-type beings. Over time the popular image of the familiar shifted to that of some kind of imp or lesser demon that could shapeshift into another form, often that of an animal. These spirits were considered evil and, in the guise of an animal, would work with witches to cause trouble and harm, or so it was thought by medieval witch hunters. The confessions of many accused witches include lurid details of mischief that demonic animal-shaped familiars incited and participated in.

It is the image of the witch and their animal companion that has prevailed and imprinted deeply into pop culture, media, literature, and the neo-Pagan movement. In Western modern witchcraft practices, many of us relate to the idea or reality that the animals around us, domestic or wild, are capable of maintaining a constructive magical relationship with us. I will agree that this is possible, but also rare. For your reference, a guide to the types of familiars associated with witches can also be found in part 1, along with some stories of the types of magic and mischief they are associated with. The language we use is in constant change, and the word *familiar* is one that is changing in usage. It is common for modern witches to use this word as a way to refer to their pets. This has become a significant and affectionate way of expressing deep feelings of connection with a beloved pet and that is fair enough. I would offer that a true familiar relationship is a type of animal-human connection that goes beyond affection and basic companionship. I will break down the terms in chapter 1 and go into detail about the differences between pets, animal companions, and animal familiars.

In part 2 we will flash forward to the witchcraft of today and take a look at the practical ways we can understand and form magical relationships with the animals in our lives. Working with an animal companion or familiar involves taking a leap into their world and learning how they perceive the worlds we share. It can be difficult to set aside our human assumptions and look through the eyes of nonhuman beings, but if we don't, we run the risk of becoming deluded or of anthropomorphizing animals. Many of us who practice modern forms of witchcraft are very drawn to the animal kingdom and the natural world as a whole. We want to connect to the unseen elements of nature and explore the hidden realms around us. I will offer ideas and ways that can help us change our perspectives about the world and attune ourselves with the perceptual realities of other creatures.

To work with the concept of the animal familiar or animal companion today is to understand that other living creatures do possess their own way of perceiving the world around them. Each species on earth has its own unique ability to process their environment, and all of these ways of perceiving lay alongside each other. For a witch to become aware of another being's ability to perceive the world increases that witch's own awareness beyond their limited human ability. What can be learned from another creature when you value them for what they truly are and what their perspective on the world is? Modern witchcraft offers us the option to blend what we can learn from science, natural history, and our own magical traditions and paths to create a workable system for creating the change we want to see in this world. Animals, both physical and in spirit, can be effective allies in this cause.

In part 3 we get into the "craft" part of witchcraft and roll up our sleeves to do, make, and create things to enhance our magical relationships with animals. How do you like to nurture and care for the creatures of the world? How can you craft those interests into a fulfilling magical practice? What are the tools involved? I love witchy lore and stories of fantastic adventures between the worlds of the seen and unseen as much as the next witch, but I also believe that witchcraft needs to be active, involved, and practical; it needs to work. Meditations, spells, correspondences, and rituals are included for you to try and experiment with.

And Then There Was Oban

Along the way I will include stories about the magical animals, both physical and in spirit, that I have known. The most significant creature in my life so far has been that special dog that taught me so much and opened my eyes to the possibility of a magical relationship with an animal. Oban was called Oban the Wonderdog for good reason. He had a startling ability to sense energy. He could sense the perimeter of a circle when it was cast and would often sit along its edge and participate in ritual along with the other witches who would come to our house to celebrate a sabbat or esbat. He could detect spirits and malevolent energy and would be a fierce guardian if something unpleasant was about.

Oban died on July 23, 2017, at the ripe old age of sixteen, but I still feel his presence quite strongly when there is magic being worked and circle being cast. He was a remarkable partner on so many adventures, magical and mundane. He was an excellent teacher of so many things to me, and I cherish the lessons I learned from him.

Without Oban I would never have been able to write a book like this one because without him I would not have been challenged to try to see the visible and invisible worlds from his point of view. I was a witch already when I adopted Oban, but he made me a better one, a more perceptive one, and I think a more compassionate and empathetic one. I hope that sharing these ideas and experiences with you continues his legacy and enriches your own experiences with the magical animals in your life.

CHAPTER ONE
Defining the Terms

How do we describe the animals—both physical and nonphysical—in our lives? Words matter, and how we use them wields power. I find it hard to put into words the incredible bond I have had with the animals I have lived with because those relationships are so pure, so sweet, and so intimate. Finding the right way to refer to the nonphysical animals I have met on the astral plane, that I have meditated, journeyed, or worked magic with, has been easier—almost. What do you call those animals that you have a magical connection with? Given that there are many types of relationships between magic practitioners and animals that have been well documented throughout history, it may help to lay them out in effort to understand them. Different types of spirits each have their own character, and there is some nuance to consider when discussing them. There is also some language that is rather loaded, so let's get started by defining some terms and clarifying a few things.

Witchcraft Animals

Throughout this book I will refer to three types of animals: pets, animal companions, and animal familiars. I make these distinctions in order to avoid confusion and clearly delineate between the living and breathing animals in our lives and the animals we work with in spirit form. Of the three terms, only one, *animal familiar*, refers to an animal in spirit form. This term honours the historic association between witches and their spirit allies and makes it explicit that these are spirits in animal form. Pets and animal companions are the physical animals in our lives, and it is how we interact with them—and their magical aptitude—that makes them different. For the sake of clarity, this is what I mean.

Pet

These are the beloved animals that live with us. They share our home and are a part of our daily life. They are not magically inclined, but just like not every human has the disposition or interest in practicing witchcraft or magic, not every animal is suited to being a practitioner either. This is not a negative thing, and there is no such thing as being "just a pet!" These creatures are our reliable friends and have the capacity to love unconditionally (or at least tolerate us reasonably) and deserve our best care and respect.

Animal Companion

These are the animals we live with that possess the rare gift of being able to interact with us on a magical level. We share a type of uncanny psychic bond and the ability to communicate beyond usual animal-human relationships with animal companions. These creatures have a sense for magical work and actively seek out opportunities to share in our workings in a mutually beneficial way. They may be able to translate messages from the unseen world to us or provide protection or insight into our magic-related activities and celebrations.

Animal Familiar

These are the nonphysical animals that act as guides, informants, and protectors for us. These may appear to us in dreams, while journeying, during ritual, in meditation, or through channelled messages or divination. I am making a point of distinguishing that these are *animal* familiars, as some of us may also have other types of beings acting as familiars, but I will include mythical beasts such as dragons, unicorns, and phoenixes as animal familiars as well.

Why Not Spirit Animals?

Within the New Age, neo-Pagan, and modern witchcraft movements, we do indeed have traditions that include animal spirits as guides, allies, and informants. There are also many traditions belonging to cultures around the world—both living ones and extinct ones—that include working with animal spirits. In most cases these animal spirits have names or titles that are part of these traditions, and we will have a look at those later in this chapter. So then—what is the problem with calling these entities our "spirit animals"? Why is this term considered offensive?

I am sure we can all agree by now that dressing up like "an Indian" is a completely inappropriate thing to do for Halloween and that wearing a warbonnet-style headdress to a rock festival is just plain wrong. We understand that these are disrespectful things to do because conversations have been held in various forums and the offensive nature of these acts has been explained. Indigenous voices have spoken up and educated non-Indigenous folks on what constitutes disrespect and appropriation. Fortunately, many of those outside of Indigenous communities are beginning to listen and understand that when the symbols and customs of other cultures are appropriated and misused, the people of those cultures are offended and hurt.

Spirit animal may be a common term, and it may sound innocent enough, but the way that this term has been used by modern, mostly white, practitioners of New Age and Pagan spiritualities has conflated it with the spiritual and religious practices of North American Indigenous peoples. This trivializes and generalizes the actual beliefs and practices of Indigenous peoples and the variety of belief systems practiced by still-living cultures.[7]

For many of us who live on land that was colonized and appropriated from the original people who lived there, or come from cultures responsible for colonization, I will maintain that it would serve us better to respect those Indigenous cultures and cease appropriating words, symbols, and practices and manipulating them to fit our own purposes. There are many Indigenous practices that were banned by colonizers, and that Indigenous people were persecuted for, that are now being appropriated, packaged, and profited from by non-Indigenous people. Despite attempts to erase them, these cultures have fought to survive.

Seldom do we consider how our actions affect the land and indwelling spirits that we, as magical practitioners, hope to work with. These beings have had relationships with the Indigenous peoples of the land for thousands of years, and I wonder how interested they are in lending their energy to fulfilling requests made by people who show disrespect for the people with whom they have a long-standing relationship? For those of us who practice magic and often rely

---

7. Smithsonian books in association with the National Museum of the American Indian, Smithsonian Institution, *Do All Indians Live in Tipis?*, 45.

on the earth to supply us with the energy and resources we need to do so, this is not a kind, good, or ethical thing to do.

When the term *spirit animal* appears in pop-culture contexts, it is often accompanied by images of Indigenous people and/or regalia in degrading, dehumanizing, and insulting situations. If you are a social media user, then you can probably picture what I am talking about and may have encountered the various quizzes to determine what your "spirit animal" is—complete with the cheesy images of a bear in a warbonnet or a scantily clad Indigenous woman with a raven on her shoulder. This imagery undermines the real relationships that Indigenous peoples have had with animals and nature for thousands of years. This also perpetuates the myth that all Indigenous people in North America have this sort of relationship with animals and that there is one homogenous Indigenous spirituality or religion.

Another reason to stop using this term is because there are Indigenous voices asking for this to stop. Representatives of the living traditions concerned have spoken up that this is offensive. It only takes one quick google search to find not only many examples of this request but to also find the offensive ways in which these words are used.

Words to Use

We are fortunate that there is no shortage of words that can be used to describe animals in spirit form. The variety of words available actually gives us a wide and rich selection of different, nuanced terms that we can use to accurately communicate the type of relationship we have with nonphysical animals without falling into appropriative or disrespectful behaviour. Let's have a look at some of them.

Charge

In the medieval times throughout Western Europe, a system of design called heraldry was used to easily identify knights on the battlefield. In the heat of combat, these images could help fighters determine friend from foe. These heraldic designs would include a charge—an object or animal selected for its symbolism and what that said about the history and identity of the individual or family represented by the heraldic image. Animals were a very popular motif, and they could be as common as a domestic cat, fierce and imposing like a lion, or as docile as a hare. Mythological beasts were used; dragons, griffins, and manticores were common choices. All of these creatures represented something important to know about the bearer of the symbol. For example, an eagle stood for power and nobility, a badger represented endurance and tenacity, and a stag stood for longevity and wisdom. These creatures are also seen in the coats of arms or clan crests of families, states, or institutions, and the symbolism is pretty consistent. You may choose to refer to a significant animal as your charge and include it in imagery you have around your personal space. If you feel that the qualities of the creature represent you as you see yourself, you could wear a charm or pendent featuring this animal as a personal protective charm or include the image as a sort of personal logo.

Daemon

In Greek mythology a daemon is the personified spirit of an abstract concept or human condition. They can be considered a minor deity or supernatural being that is the complete embodiment of the condition or concept that they represent. For example, Phobos was the daemon of panic and fear, and from him we get the word *phobia*, which means an overwhelming and excessive fear of something. We derive the word *geriatric* from the name of the daemon Geras, the personified spirit of old age who was depicted as a wizened little man, bent and stooped with age. The daemon of sleep is Hypnos. Traveling through the sky with his mother, Nyx, the goddess of night, he is the brother of Thanatos, daemon of death.

For all of these daemons, they have but one dominant purpose that is the totality of their function. They *are* what their name indicates. When your own drive for something makes you hyper focus on that one thing, it could be said that the daemon of that concept is representing you or that you are representing it. There is room to have some fun with this. You could declare that chocolate and tacos are your daemons if your hunger and craving for them drives you into a single-minded determination to eat them. If you are a devoted fan of a particular band or musician, like I am, and your fandom leads you to go to extreme lengths to catch a concert, you may claim that they are your daemon. In this sense the object of your adoration has become a personification of something very personal and intimate, a part of your soul.

Familiar

This is the term that has historically belonged to witches and the one we will discuss at length throughout this book. What started out historically as a way to describe an entity from the spirit realm that guides, advises, and informs the witch and aids them in their craft has morphed over the centuries into a cute term to describe our pets. Traditionally some familiars appear in a human-like shape, much like the popular vision of angels. Some lore describes familiars as spirits that assume the form of an animal and appear as companions to witches. It was perceived threat that led to domestic animals such as dogs and cats being killed during the witch hunts in Europe for fear of them being agents of the Devil.

While not all witches will necessarily have spirit beings guiding, protecting, or keeping them company, I would reckon that a majority of us have had, at least at one point in our lives, an animal companion who has lived with us and influenced our lives in some way. I like using the word *familiar* because it is a word that has a history with witchcraft and is ours to use. Witchcraft does have a language of its own and many words that only ever really come up when discussing it, such as *coven*, *athame*, and *widdershins* for example. We enrich and preserve our craft when we celebrate the things it provides for us and using its language is a powerful way to celebrate.

Fetch

The fetch is considered to be an embodiment of a part of the witch's true primal soul, possessing the instinct, emotion, and intuition of the one who projects it. It may even be thought of as an empty vessel that gets filled by an astral projection of the witch. Through their fetch a witch has a connection to this physical world, the Underworld, and the Dreamworld, as well as the ability to move through time and space in ways that the human form cannot.

In some folklore a person's fetch may appear when they are trying to send a crucial message or call for help—or even at the time of their death, revealing itself to the loved ones of the recently deceased as a message that they have died. In these examples the fetch appears as a doppelgänger of the person, walking silently, acting as if distracted or spaced out, and then vanishing around a corner or into the distance without a trace.

When the fetch appears in animal form, it can be one as classic as a cat or toad, something exotic like a tiger, or even a mythological creature such as a dragon or phoenix. In these cases, the animal can either be determined by a type of creature that is significant to the witch or inspired by something deep in the witch's subconscious, something they need to understand about themselves or convey to whoever else may see it.

Fylgja (pronounced FILG-ya; the plural is pronounced FILG-yur)

These creatures are the Norse take on familiar spirits and can take on human or animal forms. The word *fylgja* translates to "follower," and it does seem that the role of these spirits is to be a companion more than a guide or teacher. The animal forms they take have a strong connection to the ancestral line of the person they are attached to and may represent that person's entire family going back for generations. An animal fylgja may appear in the physical world apart from their human as a way to call for help or appear in the dreams of their person as a messenger. The human and the fylgja are bonded and linked; what happens to one happens to the other. The human's spirit may also take on the same shape as the animal fylgja when journeying.

Genius Loci

The term *genius loci* comes from classical Roman times, when these entities were seen as embodiments of the natural feature itself. This type of spirit is a spirit of a place, usually a natural one. This could be a specific location, such as a mountain, forest, or meadow, or a more expansive one, such as a country, ocean, or range of mountains. These spirits can be sensed and communed with fairly easily and can be apparent to just about anyone who shows respect for the place and has the patience to be quiet and still and pay attention to the signs and signals from them. While these spirits do not necessarily take on animal forms, they do protect and represent the natural realms in which animals live and have a relationship with them in that sense.

Mascot

Although the word *mascot* is most commonly used these days to describe a person dressed up in a costume to entertain at sporting events, the way it is used does have some significant symbolism behind it that is helpful to magical practitioners.

In the sporting example, a mascot is usually an animal (real or a person in a furry suit) that represents a team and brings it luck. The presence of this costumed ally on the sidelines is a morale booster, inspiring, entertaining, and raising energy around the desire to win the game or tournament. In the magical context, a mascot can represent you or your coven, kindred, group, or even family in a way that does the same things—inspiring and motivating you and your companions under a united image to pull together and triumph. A mascot can be chosen for its symbolism. For example, a lion may be chosen for its ferocity and bravery, an owl for its wisdom, or a cheetah for its speed.

Totem

A totem can be a natural object, a plant, or most famously an animal that is used as a symbol or emblem to represent a clan or family. The people in the group are considered to be united through a common connection with a specific totem, and it represents qualities and abilities that the associated people possess. It may even be considered as a common ancestor to the group. A totem is chosen based on something significant that happened or is believed to have happened within the shared history of the group and usually has a deep spiritual significance. The root of the word *totem* is *doodem*,[8] which comes from the Ojibwe language and refers to the clan or kinship group.

Tutelary

Tutelary is another handy word for witches to use as it refers to a spirit, deity, or one who serves as a guardian or protector over a person (or people), place, or thing. An appropriate alternative to *spirit animal* could be that the animal that watches over you is your tutelary animal. You may also use it to describe the protective relationship you have with an ancestor spirit by saying something like "My late grandmother still watches over me; she is my tutelary spirit." It was common in the Graeco-Roman period for cities to have at least one tutelary deity. Athens was named after its tutelary, Athena, and Rome had no fewer than three tutelaries with Juno, Minerva, and Jupiter. The word *patron* can be used interchangeably

---

8. "=doodem-," the Ojibwe People's Dictionary, accessed April 29, 2022, https://ojibwe.lib.umn.edu/main-entry/doodem-nad.

with *tutelary* as the meaning is very similar. Patron generally refers to a saint in this usage, while tutelary can be a deity or spirit.

* * *

As you can see, there are some good descriptive options on the table, with enough variety to suit many usages and situations, that we can choose from without falling back to using *spirit animal*. Some of these terms are historic witchcraft words, which is particularly exciting.

Working with the Terms

Pop culture has evolved the word *familiar* to mean something like "witch's pet." I will maintain that a witch's pet is a *pet* and that a witch's magical pet, which is capable of interacting on a magical level with the witch, is their *animal companion*. To say you have a familiar could mean you have a spirit ally in any form, so to be specific about an animal spirit ally, saying *animal familiar* is most helpful.

When it comes to living and working with pets, animal companions, and animal familiars there are a number of practical, spiritual, and magical elements to consider. If your animal is an actual physical one, you will want to make sure that you have the resources to properly care for their well-being and ensure that your pet or animal companion is happy, healthy, and appropriately stimulated for the best life possible. If you are working with an animal familiar, for your own peace of mind, you will want to ensure that the relationship remains healthy and free of unrealistic expectations or delusion. Check in with yourself to make sure that you are not being drained or disconnected from reality by the relationship and that you have clear boundaries in place for when it is appropriate to work and communicate with your animal familiar. This should be an exchange that enriches your spiritual and magical practice and your regular mundane life, not diminish it.

CHAPTER TWO
A Look at the Past

There is no doubt that many of us who practice magic and witchcraft value and appreciate the companionship of animals in our lives, and indeed, we may even find ways to include animals in our rituals, celebrations, and spells. Witches operate in between the worlds, beyond the boundaries of the mundane and common, so why not invite nonhuman real-life creatures to be present and help us weave our magic? It seems to flow quite nicely when a witch relates to an animal as easily as relating to another human.

I wouldn't be surprised if many of us would say that we feel more comfortable relating to other creatures that are not human—I know that I often retreat to the peace and comfort of the company of my dogs when things get stressful or too hectic in the day-to-day grind of my life. The unconditional and non-judgemental nature of my two sweet, energetic, and hilarious dogs brings me closer to the better aspects of my life and also of myself. This is the part of me that I prefer to nurture—the part of me that loves to amble along riverbanks, explore wooded areas, and lie on the soft summer grass. My dogs love it too, so they become my motivation for doing those things, propelling me to get out and move my body, enjoy the fresh air, and indulge all three of us in what we love to do. My dogs allow me to be who I really am, to be my natural witch self without judgement or attitude. They join me when I stop to admire a pretty rock, they sniff the flowers and investigate the foliage right along beside me, and we stand three abreast, stock-still, when we happen upon the frequent deer grazing in our neighbourhood. This close kinship and mutual appreciation of the things that spark curiosity and wonder in all three of us, to me, is a kind of magic in itself. How could I not think of Lola and Georgia, my canine companions, as anything but my allies in magic?

I am willing to bet that we have all read or heard stories about animal helpers that guide and aid their human companions. We see in stories from around the world, and in many different contexts, a trusty and clever animal that is the faithful and intuitive companion to the story's hero. Why is it then that the animal companions of witches, which we shall refer to as animal familiars, are so reviled? How did these malevolent minions of Satan that accompanied the witches of old become the present-day pampered fur babies I see posted by practitioners on social media?

In order to set the stage, I will start with a brief history of animal familiars as they relate to modern-day practitioners of witchcraft, particularly those of us who follow neo-Pagan paths and witchcraft traditions inspired by British- and European-style traditions. The way we use the term *familiar* has evolved over time and has broadened to have several connotations, but the general spirit of the word remains the same.

Familiar of the Gods

Some of the earliest myths and legends of the gods also include their animal companions, and these stories often influence how we, as devotees of the old gods, form relationships with these same animals. For example, Hugin and Munin are the ravens who act as informants for the Norse god Odin. Hugin, who represents thought, and Munin, who represents memory, fly across Midgard (earth) to gather intelligence and spy on Odin's enemies and then return to Asgard, where Odin lives, to report all that they have learned. Indeed, it is very common for gods to have a constant and reliable animal companion to work with, and through the depictions of their relationships with these animals, we learn more about the gods themselves. The animals become extensions of the gods' personalities, making them more relatable and real to us. We get to see how the relationship between god and animal makes the god somehow stronger and wiser, their powers enhanced by the cunning and natural abilities of the beast. Odin needs Hugin and Munin in order to gather the intelligence he needs. The ravens represent aspects of Odin's mind and intellect—his thought and memory. He is a god of war and death, and ravens are carrion eaters, known to feast on the bodies of the slain. When Odin decides who dies in battle, the ravens are there to clear the battlefield of death. The reciprocal relationship that Odin has with

Hugin and Munin uses the inherent nature of the birds to enrich his work. By observing and understanding the mythical relationships the gods have with their animal companions, we can understand what our own relationships with animals can be.

Like Odin, the Greek god Zeus also had a winged companion in the form of a giant golden eagle named Aquila. This eagle was revered for his powerful wings and natural ability to fly to great heights. As such a powerful bird, he was enlisted to carry the god's thunderbolts and was also sent by Zeus to carry the beautiful mortal Ganymede up to Olympus to serve the gods as a cup-bearer. Aquila remains in the heavens to this day as a constellation of the same name. It can be found in close proximity to the constellation of Aquarius, which represents Ganymede, forever swooping in on the cup-bearing youth. Zeus's relationship with Aquila has become part of the mythology that helps us understand our night sky and position of the stars. The metaphors and symbols of this story informs the astrology that many witches and metaphysical practitioners use as a tool to this day. The heavens contain a cast of other creatures that have stars, constellations, and heavenly bodies named after them, and this body of lore adds to this rich toolbox for understanding our place in the world.

The Greek goddess Hecate has several recorded animal companions, but it is her association with dogs that is most renowned. Her canine companions guard the gates of the Underworld and serve as messengers, delivering messages to humans from the dark goddess. The appearance of Hecate is heralded by the sound of dogs baying and barking, and she is known to shapeshift into the form of a dog. It makes sense that Hecate would employ the natural instinct of her hounds to guard and protect and assist her in her work. Hecate's hounds are effective at guarding the gates to the Underworld because this is what dogs will do. Even the smallest of dogs (and I see this with my wee, 13-pound Georgia) will defend the territory of their pack, be it canine, human, or divine. The canine intelligence is keen and eager to please, so loyally serving their pack leader by performing tasks is completely on brand; they aim to please. Through the power of a witch's imagination and visualization, we, too, can shapeshift into the form of a dog to give us the fierceness and determination to stay on task and get our work done. You can look to the example of Hecate for clues and guidance in how to make this work.

In chapter 4 of this book, I will offer a closer look at the relationships of particular deities and their animal companions and explore ways in which this can inform your own magical practice.

Familiar to Humans

The relationship between a witch and their familiar is an extension of the age-old relationship between human beings and animals—with the added bonus being that witches have the added layers of perception to work with animals in. The Upper World is the realm of gods and spirits, where we can relate to the divine aspects of animal energy and relationships. In the Lower World, or Underworld, the realm of birth, death, and rebirth; our ancestors; and souls, we can relate to the transformative aspects of animal relationships. Here, where we live in the Middle World, our physical and mundane reality, we can explore the advantages of having constructive and enriching real-life relationships with animals. I will dive into this in greater detail in part 2 of this book, but for now let's take a look at that bond between humans and animals and where it comes from.

Human beings have been attracted to relationships with animals since time began. While it is true that the primary driver for this relationship was survival and hunting, we also have relied on them for other equally important life-affirming reasons—namely companionship and, for those of us who are inclined, the connection that they give us to the nonhuman and spirit worlds. We can see this fascination emerge in the art that our distant ancestors created. Of all the things early humans could have depicted in prehistoric art, animals have been a reoccurring subject in cave paintings across the globe. From the famous Lascaux cave paintings in France, estimated to be about 20,000 years old,[9] to the Sulawesi cave paintings in Indonesia, dating back at least 45,500 years,[10] animals are the main subject of many works.

Human beings are one of the very few creatures on the planet that will adopt and nurture other animals. Our earliest ancestors would have looked at the animals around them not just as opportunities for food but as powerful allies, capable of doing things that humans could not do, with wisdom and knowledge that could be learned from. Three key behaviours have dictated human

---

9. Clottes, "The Lascaux Cave Paintings."
10. Brumm et al., "Oldest Cave Art Found in Sulawesi."

evolution: tool making, the invention of spoken and symbolic language, and the domestication of plants and animals. According to anthropologist Pat Shipman, there is a fourth behaviour, which she refers to as "animal connection," and she offers that this has been the underlying link joining the first three behaviours throughout human history for the last 2.6 million years.[11] Shipman's hypothesis states that humans have been intimately and persistently connected with animals throughout history and that our evolution and adaptative changes have been linked to this animal connection. We developed tools in order to hunt and protect ourselves from animals, we developed language and symbols to communicate information relating to the behaviour and movement of animals, and then finally we domesticated animals, first as living tools, aiding in hunting and protection, then as livestock and food.

From these ancient roots an inherently human impulse to live and work with animals has been maintained. A sympathy and connection to the animals made us more and more human. The deepest needs of our bodies, minds, and spirits became inexplicably linked to the other animals on the planet. The needs of our bodies for food drove hunting and animal husbandry, and the needs of our minds and spirits for connection to unseen worlds led us to follow the animals into their secret realms for a closer connection to the raw forces of nature, magic, and the gods. It is from this impulse, an impulse to be intimately linked to the intelligence of the animals and see our world through eyes other than our own, that the witch's familiar evolved.

The witch's familiar classically appears in animal form, but other nonanimal examples have been recorded for other types of magic workers. An Arabic grimoire of occult magic and astrology called the *Ghāyat al-Hakīm* (*The Goal of the Wise*), better known in the West as the *Picatrix*, credits a sage named Caraphzebiz as being the founder of this type of magic and the first person to have a relationship with a familiar spirit. Dating from the tenth or eleventh century, this grimoire quotes Aristotle as stating that through working with his familiar spirit, Caraphzebiz become a sage and gained his knowledge of nature and science. His familiar spirit is quoted as saying to him: "I will remain with you, but do not reveal me to others or speak of me and make sacrifices in my name."[12]

11. Shipman, "The Animal Human Connection and Human Evolution."
12. Greer and Warnock, *The Complete Picatrix*, 152.

Here we see an early reference to three key features of working with a familiar that witches are associated with: the idea that familiars could teach or inform, that the relationship was to be discreet and private, and that they require their human to make offerings or in some way sacrifice to them.

Early Modern Familiars & Their Witches

It was during the early modern period (1500–1700 CE) that the image of the witch and their familiar that we would recognize today became popular. During the witch hunts of the early modern period, when the persecution of witches was at its height across Europe and Great Britain, it was recorded in the trial records of some of the condemned that they had a demonic familiar in the form of an animal. These demons were believed to be malevolent spirits or imps that could transform into the shape of animals such as toads, rats, mice, insects, dogs, cats, and birds. Occasionally it would be reported that a particular familiar was able to shapeshift into multiple animal forms.

It is important to understand that although there were many cases in which people were accused of witchcraft, it is unlikely that the vast majority of the accused were actually witches, and certainly not witches as many of us self-identify as today. A general fear of witchcraft permeated European society at the time, and it became a trend to accuse people who were different in some way of being involved in these diabolic arts. Being wealthy, attractive, possessing an envious talent, or doing just about anything that could be construed by the neighbours as "suspicious" could earn a hapless person an accusation of witchcraft.

It is from the trial records of this period that we also collect some data on which animals were most often identified as witches' familiars. Between the years 1530 and 1712, there were approximately 322 cases in which animal-related evidence was presented in England (the exact number is hard to pinpoint due to the unreliable way the records were taken and kept).[13] The largest group of familiars referred to are nondescript, being referred to by their alleged deeds or their names. The actual animals that were named, listed here in descending order of popularity, were cats, dogs, toads, wild birds, poultry, moles, and rats. This list is fascinating and also quite relatable to the types of animals that modern witches would consider as familiars today.

---

13. Serpell, "Guardian Spirits or Demonic Pets," 157–90.

One early example of an accused witch cavorting around with an animal familiar can be found in the case of Dame Alice Kyteler, an Irish woman living in Kilkenny in 1324. She is the first recorded person in Ireland to be tried and condemned for witchcraft and only managed to survive because she was able to flee the country and live out her days in England.[14] Alice was a wealthy and successful woman, and she had been married four times during her colourful life. She was accused of witchcraft by some of her stepchildren, who had not received the inheritances they were due when their fathers mysteriously died, apparently by poisoning.

Alice was accused of sorcerous acts along with a group of alleged followers and charged with a number of diabolic crimes. Of Alice, it was said:

> **The said dame had a certain demon, an incubus, named Son of Art, or Robin son of Art, who had carnal knowledge of her, and from whom she admitted that she had received all her wealth. This incubus made its appearance under various forms, sometimes as a cat, or as a hairy black dog.[15]**

In reviewing the court records and documents of the time there are many details of familiars that repeat from case to case, and they often echo the three key features that were mentioned in the *Picatrix*. The idea of sacrifice to the familiar, in the form of feeding it, was mentioned often. The witch was said to have a mark, spot, or sometimes an extra nipple from which the familiar would suck the blood of the witch. In his 1597 dissertation on the lore of witchcraft of the time, titled *Daemonologie*, King James IV of Scotland, an ardent believer in the perceived threat of witchcraft, spirits, and magic, included the confessions of a young woman named Phillip Flower, who, along with her mother, Joane, and sister Margret, was accused of being involved in the mysterious death of Frances, Earl of Rutland. According to this record:

> **She confesses and says, that she has a Spirit sucking on her in the form of a white Rat, which keeps her left breast, and has so done for three or four years, and concerning the agreement between her**

---

14. Seymour, *Irish Witchcraft and Demonology*, 58.
15. Seymour, *Irish Witchcraft and Demonology*, 42.

Spirit and herself, she confesses and says, that when it first came to her, she gave her Soul to it, and promised to do her good, and cause Thomas Simpson to love her, if she would suffer it to suck her, which she agreed to.[16]

It was often the familiar who sought the witch, simply approaching them and offering them a service in exchange for food, shelter, or a favour in return. Witches could also inherit their familiar from another family member or witch. A group of witches might have a familiar in common, sharing responsibility for the familiar's care and feeding. The familiar was attached to the witch by the strength of their relationship and the bond created by working together but was not "owned" by the witch. They maintained a sense of autonomy and could also choose to abandon the relationship if the witch did not meet their needs, taking with them any services that the witch would be benefitting from.

Voice of the Devil

People accused of witchcraft in the early modern period notoriously made pacts with the Devil, or so claimed contemporary reports. These alleged pacts were well documented through court records and pamphlets, and the accused witches were often led to confess to this through the torture they endured at the hands of their inquisitors. This may not be the most reliable way to get information, but the repeated patterns in these confessions suggest that there was something within the popular culture of the period that made these types of stories reappear in confessions time and time again. The Devil would often appear in animal form, most often as a goat, and the witches would confess to kissing his ass to seal their pact. It was from the Devil that some witches received their familiars, and the Devil may even have given them a name.

The familiar could provide a means for the witch to communicate directly with the Devil. The familiar, in the form of a domestic animal—a dog, cat, or rat, for example—could move about freely and pass messages or collect intelligence for the witch without drawing attention to itself, in theory anyway. It was the very presence of these domestic animals in the homes of common people that built evidence for a charge of witchcraft against them in some cases. This

---

16. King James, *The Annotated Daemonologie, The Wonderful Discoverie of Witchcraft*, 150.

was a time in history when it was not as common as it is now to have an animal just as a pet. Keeping a pet was an expensive indulgence, and many animals had to have a practical function in order to earn their keep. Livestock could be eaten and produced goods such as wool, milk, or eggs. Beasts of burden provided transportation or could pull a plough. For people of more privileged classes, a hunting dog or falcon could be employed. For a person to have an animal live with them in a domestic situation was not unheard of, but it was less common, and it could draw suspicion, especially if other unusual things had been noticed about that person.

The Criminalization of Familiars

King James IV had become actively invested in uncovering witchcraft and rooting it out of his kingdom. In 1590 he was to marry Anne of Denmark, a marriage that would provide the all-important heir to the throne and reinforce James's authority as ruling monarch. When a series of storms prevented Anne from traveling from Denmark, James mounted an expedition to bring her to Scotland personally. Accompanied by an entourage of some three hundred men, James sailed to fetch Anne. The voyage back to Scotland was difficult, and they were faced with terrible storms while at sea. James became convinced that these storms were sent by witches as part of a diabolical plot to kill him and his bride. This resulted in the North Berwick Witch Trials, in which approximately sixty people were accused of witchcraft. James was a devoted Protestant and believed that he, as "God's lieutenant" on earth, ruled by divine will. In a pamphlet published in 1591, *Newes from Scotland*, it was reported that the witches accused of plotting against James asked the Devil himself why it was that he hated James: "At which time the witches demanded of the devil why he did bear such hatred to the King, who answered, by reason the King is the greatest enemy he hath in the world."[17]

For the king it was imperative to be seen as being firmly on the side of God, acting on God's behalf and fighting the forces of evil. Throughout the reigns of Henry VIII and Elizabeth I, there were a number of acts against the practice of witchcraft in general that were passed. Upon the death of Elizabeth I in 1603, James IV of Scotland became James I of England. His power and influence

---

17. "Newes from Scotland. Declaring the Damnable Life and Death of Doctor Fian a Notable Sorcerer, Who Was Burned at Edenbrough in Ianuarie Last. 1591."

had expanded into new territory and expanded his obsession for persecuting witches. The new king united the kingdoms of Scotland, Ireland, and England, and he proclaimed himself the King of Great Britain in 1604. That same year he also introduced a significant act against witchcraft entitled An Act against Conjuration, Witchcraft and Dealing with Evil and Wicked Spirits. In this piece of law, it is notable that the practice of working with a familiar is specifically named, criminalized, and made punishable by death. It clearly states:

> **That if any person or persons, after the said Feast of St. Michael the Archangel next coming, shall use, practise, or exercise any invocation or conjuration of any evil and wicked spirit: or shall consult, covenant with, entertain, employ, feed, or reward any evil and wicked spirit, to or for any intent or purpose.**[18]

Even within this act we see the reappearance of the three key features of the relationship between a human and their familiar. The act is explicitly stating that it is a crime punishable by death to "consult, covenant with, entertain, employ, feed, or reward" these familiars. It is not surprising then that the trial records of the period would contain explicit details of accused witches having relationships with familiars, as this would be the kind of evidence that the courts would be actively seeking to secure a conviction on.

But why were people so easily led into believing that these animals could act as familiars and do the supernatural deeds that they were believed to do? Much of what we understand today about the witchcraft of this period comes from three main sources: the laws that were being enforced at the time, the court records of the trials, which will be biased by the attitude of the court and/or the church, and from pamphlets that were written at the time for distribution to the public. These pamphlets were a huge influence on how the citizens would learn and then talk about witches, their practices, and also their familiars. Like any other tabloid, the journalism was questionable and likely much more colourful than what really had happened.

Looking back on the 1604 act against witchcraft by King James I, he is very specific about what exactly was involved in the crime of witchcraft, so we can

---

18. "1604: 1 James 1 c.12."

assume that he was responding to a threat that he was already convinced of. The language of the law itemizes very specific behaviour and distinctly calls out working with familiar spirits. King James was targeting a specific practice that was believed to be in opposition to his religion, and he was determined to root it out. On the surface, the image of the witch relating to their familiar was not all that different from the depiction of animal companions in the folklore or biblical lore of the time. What made the critical and often fatal difference was that the witch and their familiar were demonized. Instead of being a benevolent messenger, the familiar became a diabolical informant, capable of nefarious deeds, and the witch was their servant or their master.

It might be easy to jump to the conclusion that the familiars associated with the witches of this period were an invention of the Christian churches as a way to squash out witches and any lingering traces of pre-Christian religion. But the answer to this is still evolving, and as more and more information comes to light through academic research, the story is becoming more nuanced than that. While there have been documented cases of familiars in various animal forms around the world, it is in Great Britain, specifically in England, that the highest number of documented animal familiars on record are found.[19] It is in these stories that we see the recognizable imagery and associations of familiars that we have in modern witchcraft and popular culture today.

Familiars and Fairies

The reality is that the fascination and belief in familiars did not sprout up out of nowhere, and once it touched popular culture of early modern England, it grew strong and held on. This may be due, in part, to an existing framework of belief that was relatable to the population and was easy to make the leap into believing.

Throughout the British Isles, belief in fairy folklore was already deeply entrenched in the psyche of the people. Dating back to long before the arrival of Christianity on British shores, there was a common belief in fairies of many different types and descriptions that were known for all sorts of actions and behaviour, some of it helpful, some of it harmful, and everything in-between. The fair folk could usually be appeased with some sort of offering of food or drink and in return would inform or assist the human in some way. This is

19. Leddy, "One may be an Imp as well as another," 9.

parallel to the reputation of the familiar, who also required some sort of appeasement in order to form a relationship with the witch.

In the article "The Witch's Familiar and the Fairy in Early Modern England and Scotland," writer Emma Wilby examines the relationship and similarities between fairy folklore and the emergence of the lore around witches' familiars of the early modern period. Wilby offers that the old fairy beliefs became conflated with the contemporary construction of the emerging lore of the witch's familiar and highlights how the two types of spirit beings essentially have the same sort of motivation:

> Those aspects with which the familiar was primarily associated—that is, human/animal health, domestic/farming processes and the general securing of material prosperity—were also areas of central concern to many types of fairy. Conversely, certain skills which were primarily associated with the fairies—such as the ability to divine the future, seek out lost goods, identify criminals and so on—were often associated with the familiar.[20]

King James of England put this into law in the 1604 Act against Conjuration, Witchcraft and Dealing with Evil and Wicked Spirits, where he addresses some particular abilities shared by fairies and familiars and identifies them explicitly, and decrees it a crime punishable by death to:

> Take upon him or them, by Witchcraft, Inchantment, Charme, or Sorcery, to tell or declare in what place any Treasure of Golde or Silver should or might be found or had in the earth, or other secret places; or where goods, or things lost, or stolen, should be found or become, or to the intent to provoke any person to unlawful love, or whereby any Cattell, or Goods of any person shall be destroyed, wasted, or impaired; or to hurt or destroy any person in his or her body, although the same be not effected and done.[21]

---

20. Wilby, "The Witch's Familiar and the Fairy in Early Modern England and Scotland."
21. "1604: 1 James 1 c.12."

As the seventeenth century drew to a close, attitudes and laws regarding witchcraft shifted from paranoia and superstition to skepticism and disbelief. By the beginning of the eighteenth century, the hysteria of the witch hunt era in Europe and Britain was winding down and the introduction of the Witchcraft Act of 1735 mirrored these changing attitudes. It was no longer assumed that witches had diabolical pacts with the Devil and supernatural relationships with imps and demons in the form of animals. The new, "enlightened" law determined that witches were not real and anyone claiming to be a witch was a con artist looking to defraud innocent people in some way. The new law also abolished the hunting and execution of witches, opting instead to imprison anyone caught in defiance of the new rules. The act of 1735 remained in force until 1951 in Great Britain when it was replaced with the Fraudulent Mediums Act.

Throughout this period, animals appeared as speaking characters in fairy tales, fables, myths, and folklore. Oral folk tales, which had been handed down from generation to generation, began to be written down, published, and widely shared. The morality stories credited to a sixth-century BCE Greek slave, Aesop, were published for the first time in English by William Caxton in 1484 as *The Fables of Aesop*. While the fables are now generally targeted at children, the values and ethics presented in them have influenced countless people of all ages down through the centuries.

The way animals were anthropomorphized in these stories continues to influence our perception of animals to this day—the cunning fox, the clever crow, the industrious ant—and also influence how we use language. Think about popular sayings such as "slow and steady wins the race"—the lesson of *The Hare and the Tortoise*, a fable about how determination and patience can overcome a boisterous and apparently stronger opponent. Classic fables, such as the Crow and the Pitcher, use the clever behaviour of animals, in this case a crow, to teach a lesson. In the Crow and the Pitcher, a crow uses ingenuity to drink when he is thirsty, dropping stones into the deep pitcher so that the water level rises, and he can drink. In the 725 fables credited to Aesop, animals are the teachers of crucial lessons to humans.

Fairy tales, as a genre, can be traced back to 1697 when Charles Perrault, a French writer, released his collection of existing folk tales and rhymes under the title *Contes da ma Mère l'Oie* (*Tales of My Mother Goose*). An English translation by Robert Samber followed in 1729 and eventually made its way to the

United States in 1786, bringing the tales of Little Red Riding Hood and Puss in Boots, among others, to a wider and wider audience. Witches became characters in fairy tales, their influence diminished to mere entertainment, and their influence as demonic threats began to fade. Talking animals were now teaching moral lessons instead of conveying messages from the Devil.

With the dawn of the Victorian Era came a renewed interest in fairy folklore. The unprecedented change brought about by the Industrial Revolution was reinventing society and also the very landscape. People were moving from traditional rural ways of living to new urban lifestyles at an ever-increasing rate. This shift away from the romanticized simplicity of days gone by created a longing for a return to a gentler, more pastoral time. Fairy stories and fables once transmitted orally were now being galvanized in books with their hard edges smoothed off, the scary bits being eroded down to make them more child friendly. New generations of children received the words of animals, spinning and weaving their adventures across pages of these books, sparking imaginations and treating readers of all ages to fantastic stories that inspired a kind of magic of their own.

The early twentieth century saw the publication of a children's book that beautifully epitomized the desire to reconnect with nature and gave animals centre stage as our allies to help humans do this. *The Wind in the Willows* (1908) by Kenneth Grahame introduced a charming cast of sweet animals who had great adventures around the countryside, including a profound encounter with the god Pan—a story that had a deep and lasting effect on more than one modern witch.

Familiar Relationships Today

Looking back at this history, it may be a stretch to draw direct lines from the stories of the past to the types of relationships we enjoy with the pets or animal companions we have in our lives today. I am sure that if you asked just about anyone who lives with a pet, they will tell you that they are guilty of carrying on close relationships with their animals, speaking to them, caring for them, and feeding and pampering them in a way that would have drawn suspicion from the witchfinders of the early modern era. I am sure that I am not the only modern witch out there who has had profound experiences with animals that resemble the ones recorded in the witch trial records. I have certainly had the experience where I believe that an animal has spoken to me and given me information that I needed at the time. I can also attest that I have had experiences where I have witnessed something that

I would classify as an encounter with a familiar-type spirit. While I truly value these occasions when they happen, I also like to be very pragmatic with my magic, and I believe that these incidents were the exception and not the rule.

Modern witches include animals in their magical practices in a myriad of ways. We may adopt the symbol of an animal as a totem or mascot to represent ourselves and project the magical will of ourselves as individuals or our groups. We might incorporate animal images into our sacred spaces, our altars, shrines, or circles, for inspiration or protection or to honour the spirit or type of energy that the animal projects. We may make use of the body parts of animals in the creation of ritual tools or artifacts, honouring the life force that these things contain. We may cook ritual or celebratory feasts using animal products to nurture and sustain our own bodies. We may perform dances or movements that imitate animals in order to strengthen our connection to and understanding of their power and place in the natural world. The only limit to how we choose to work with animals is our own imaginations.

In working with animals, we must always consider the ethical responsibilities of our actions. Witches have long been associated with animal sacrifice and cruelty, and this is a negative stereotype that has been a scar on witchcraft communities for centuries. Some witches have responded to this by becoming animal advocates and rights activists, adopting vegetarian or vegan diets, and not using animal products in their witchcraft. Other witches embrace eating meat and using animal products in their magical practices and mundane lives. Whichever side of this issue you find yourself on, it is worth reflecting on the consequences of your actions and how your life affects the lives of the animals in your environment. As humanity becomes increasingly urban, few of us hunt and farm, and we are disconnected from the reality of the sacrifice of animals to sustain us. Animals touch our everyday life usually in two capacities—as pets or as meat, purchased from a shop far from the processing facility where their lives ended. They no longer have a spiritual or mythic context in our lives. As witches and workers of magic, we have the opportunity to re-establish that missing link of spiritual connection with animals and reinforce their historic connection to humans. We can re-examine and revive the "animal connection" that Pat Shipman wrote about. Witches and magic workers have the tools and knowledge to reconnect to the animal world and partake of their wisdom and perspective through our magic and our will to pay attention.

CHAPTER THREE
Animals in Witchcraft Folklore

Folklore is defined as customs, music, stories, and traditional beliefs that are handed down through time by word of mouth. The stories may change over time, adapt by region, and shift with societal change. Usually if you squint hard enough, you will find that golden nugget of truth or wisdom in folklore and a general lesson in the values and priorities of the culture the lore is coming from. Animals are an intrinsic part of folklore generally. In these stories, animals play many roles—as omens, messengers, heroes, villains, and even ingredients.

In compiling this chapter's list of animals and choosing the lore to be included for each, it was important to me to stick to the reason for writing this book. In my own research, reading, and understanding, the modern take on witches and their relationships with animal familiars is informed by the representation of animal familiars during the early modern period in Europe and Great Britain. It is my intention to primarily list the animals that were repeatedly mentioned as familiars in the documents pertaining to witches from this era and also expand this slightly to include key animals that are widely appealing to modern witches.

Not everyone's favourite critter is going to be in the chapter, but the usual suspects will be. Many of us, myself included, will not find our own animal familiars detailed here—no polar bears, badgers, or gerbils—but perhaps this template will inspire you to do your own research on folklore pertaining to them. Anecdotally I noticed that modern witches tend to ally themselves with animals for one of two main reasons; either they like them and have some kind of personal history with the particular animal or that animal has an association with a deity that they worship or have an affinity for. I will share more detailed information about deities and their animal companions in chapter 4, "Companions of the Gods," and I will stick with folklore for now.

Bats

In Dante's epic poem *Inferno*, we see the Devil cast with bat wings, an image that has lasted through the centuries and has contributed to the reputation of the bat as a sinister creature, in league with the evil forces of nature:

> **And the right-hand one seemed 'twixt white and yellow;**
> **The left was such to look upon as those**
> **Who come from where the Nile falls valley-ward.**
> **Underneath each came forth two mighty wings,**
> **Such as befitting were so great a bird;**
> **Sails of the sea I never saw so large.**
> **No feathers had they, but as of a bat**
> **Their fashion was and he was waving them,**
> **So that three winds proceeded forth therefrom.**[22]

Bats are liminal creatures, existing in the spaces between day and night, emerging from their lairs at twilight to swoop through the air and feed. They have wings and fly like birds, yet they are mammals that nurse their young and have furry bodies, not feathered. Bats are found almost everywhere on earth with only the Arctic, Antarctica, and a few remote islands not hosting any bat population.

There is precious little folklore pertaining to bats in Britain, but they retain a strong association with witchcraft and the occult. They are among the creatures that witches were believed to shapeshift into, their nocturnal habits and flying at night not helping their reputation. Another superstition related to witches was that if a bat was seen flying straight upwards, then immediately straight back down to the ground, it was a sign that the Witches' Hour had come. It was considered extremely unlucky if a bat should fly into a home as it was believed that this was a sign that someone living there would soon die, or in other accounts, it meant that it would rain. Bats in the house could also be interpreted as a sign that you may have bedbugs or that your visitors will soon be leaving—which would certainly happen if your guests didn't like bats! There is a Manx saying

---

22. Dante, *Inferno*, Canto XXXIV.

that goes "fine weather is certain when bats fly about at sunset." This sentiment proves that not all bat lore is negative or related to evil sorcery.

The use of bat parts in witches' brew was noted in Shakespeare's *Macbeth* when the three Weird Sisters include "wool of bat" in their bubbling cauldron.[23] Another literary reference to bats that further linked them to malevolent forces was in Bram Stoker's *Dracula*, in which the vampire is said to have the power to transform into one. This sensational connection is perhaps rooted in the existence of bats that do feed on blood. But it may disappoint vampire enthusiasts to learn that only three of the more than 1,400 species of bats actually do this.

During the medieval period, bats were sometimes referred to as "witches' birds," as bats were believed to act as familiars to witches and their blood and body parts were thought to have magical properties. It was the presence of a large number of these witches' birds flying about the residence and gardens of the unfortunate Lady Jacaume of Bayonne, France, in 1332 that caused her to be tried as a witch and publicly burned at the stake.[24]

The most repeated folklore pertaining to bats is the persistent story that bats are attracted to women's hair and will fly at it, becoming tangled and making it necessary to cut them out with scissors. This is untrue. Bats may indeed swoop close to a person's head, but that would likely be to catch insects flying nearby, not out of any attraction to hair.

Bees

Evidence of apiculture, or beekeeping, dates back to at least 2500 BCE in Egypt and could go back even further in China. Long before they figured out how to manage and control colonies of bees, our ancestors foraged for honey. A cave painting dating back to 9000 BCE near Valencia, Spain, depicts the image of a person climbing a tree to harvest honey with their hand. The clever artist of this prehistoric art even included honeybees buzzing around the intrepid forager.

Among the Celtic peoples, bees were seen as intermediaries between the spirit world and the living. They could travel to the realm of the gods, bearing messages and omens. The Irish goddess Brigid is closely associated with bees, and it was believed that the magical nectar from her apple orchard in the

---

23. Shakespeare, *Macbeth*, act IV, scene I.
24. Laird, *Bat*, 46.

Otherworld was transported to earth by her beloved bees. This theme of bees and the mysteries of death wound its way through time, sticking to the British Isles and surfacing again in the eighteenth and nineteenth centuries in the tradition of "telling the bees." In order to not offend these sensitive insects, they have to be treated as members of the family who keeps them, and as such, they must be informed of any big news or changes to the family order, such as births, marriages, or deaths. Customs vary by region but include traditions such as sharing food appropriate for the event with each hive or draping the hives with black cloth or ribbon if the family is in mourning. It was believed that each hive should be directly spoken to, informing them of the event, and some believed that a family member, often a son, should move the hives to let the bees know that a change has taken place.

The Museum of Witchcraft and Magic, located in Boscastle, United Kingdom, has a wonderful example of a bee charm in its collection. When I visited the museum in 2012, I photographed the charm, which was displayed along with a sign that read:

> **Here we have three bumble bees, put carefully in a pouch to be hung up in the best room in the house. They will bring health, happiness and good fortune to the home. A widespread Devon charm, this one was recovered in 1949 from Dawlish.**[25]

The charm is a simple one as it is, indeed, three fuzzy and round bumble bees and a simple dark blue leather pouch. Nothing else was written about this particular example in the display, but I could see how the symbol of these bees could bring health, happiness, and good fortune, as this is what bees and their two primary products, honey and wax, could impart to the household. As a witch, I could naturally see a significance to the chosen number of bees in the charm—three bees for birth, death, and rebirth; the upper, lower, and middle worlds; or any number of holy trinities you could imagine.

Another common belief, and one that I share, is that bees do not like violence or aggression of any kind. British folklore holds that bees will swarm and leave if their keepers are hostile, argumentative, or loud or if they swear. In my

---

25. The credit for this explanation was that it was "adapted from text by Cecil Williamson."

own experience around beehives, I found that they do prefer gentle and quiet actions and that I do not require a veil or protective clothing to prevent being stung if I move slowly and speak softly. The only time I was ever stung was when I was distracted and carelessly stomped past a hive, not watching for or respecting the bees around me. I painfully learned my lesson and have not been stung since.

Cats

There is no more iconic an animal companion for a witch than the cat, be it black or any other colour, and the relationship between witches and cats deserves an entire book of its own. Cats are easily one of the most common household pets in the world, and most of us, I am sure, have had a cat involved in our lives in some way. We admire them for their aloofness, their independence, and the way that they can make us feel chosen when they decide to show us affection. Cats allude a seductive, feminine grace and are easily aligned with the intuitive, dark, and mysterious realms of magic and witchcraft.

The presence of felines in the lives of humans dates well back into antiquity. From ancient Egypt to medieval Britain, cats were respected and celebrated for their mousing abilities and usefulness in protecting food stores from rodent intrusion. Before they became the target for witch hunt-related superstition and persecution, cats were welcome in monasteries in order to keep mice and rats at bay, and indeed, we can see tributes to them within the illuminated manuscripts of the time. Why, then, did cats fall from grace and become the targets of purges and persecution? Their mysterious lure and association with witchcraft and sorcery condemned cats just as it did those accused of witchcraft.

On the thirteenth of June 1233, Pope Gregory IX issued a papal bull, the Vox in Rama, detailing a satanic cult that he believed was operating in Germany. This document, sent to King Henry of Germany, included lurid details of the activities of these alleged witches. One such activity was an initiation ritual in which the participants would celebrate with a meal. After the meal, a statue of a black cat would come to life and then walk backwards with its tail erect so that the new initiate and then the leader of the group would kiss it on its backside. This would be followed by an orgy and then the appearance of Lucifer, who was described in the bull as having a lower body that was covered with fur, like a cat.[26] This accusation drew a connection between cats and witches that persisted through the ages and led to a tradition of killing cats for superstitious reasons across Europe until the 1800s.

Cats are featured as witches' familiars frequently in the trial records and documents from the witchcraft trials of the early modern period. The accused witches were said to have not only kept them as familiars but to have also shape-shifted into feline form. It is worth noting that despite cats being the most iconic of the familiar animals, hares were more common according to these same documents.

In a curious and charming book called *Beware the Cat* by William Baldwin, there is a reference to a folk superstition about cats that continues to this day. Published in the late sixteenth century and credited to be the earliest piece of long-prose fiction in the English language, the book refers to cats having nine lives. Baldwin attributes this to the relationship between cats and witches:

> **I take rather to be an Hagat or a Witch then a Cat. For witches have gone often in that likenes, And therof hath come the proverb as trew as common, that a Cat hath nine lives, that is to say, a witch may take on her a Cats body nine times.**[27]

Not just a companion for witches, cats were beloved companions for sailors as well, coming with the added bonus of providing vermin control. Cats, particularly polydactyls, were seen as good luck to have on ships; with their extra toes, they were thought to have better balance for high seas. Bad luck would follow if the ship cat fell or was thrown overboard, as this would cause storms and rough, dangerous seas. A ship that survived these storms would suffer nine years of bad luck. A cat's sneeze was an omen for rain, a frisky cat meant wind was coming up, and if a cat groomed themselves against the pattern of their fur, it meant a hailstorm was imminent.

The luck associated with cats can be conflicting. The presence of black cats in some charms brings good luck, while a black cat crossing your path may do just the opposite. The presence of a cat—alive or dead—as a good luck or protective charm was also found on land. Families of fishermen along the Yorkshire

26. Natasha, "Thou Shalt Not Suffer a Cat to Live."
27. Baldwin, *Beware the Cat*, 22.

coast of Britain would keep black cats to ensure that their menfolk would return safely from sea, and these felines were well taken care of in exchange for this favour. Concealing the bodies of dead cats in the roof, walls, or under the floorboards of a building was considered a charm to protect against malevolent witchcraft or a sort of "scarecrow" to ward off mice and rats. These felines were referred to simply as "dried cats," and examples of this grisly practice have been found throughout Ireland, Sweden, and Europe with the highest number of documented cased coming from Britain. The practice was so widespread that it migrated with colonists to the United States, Canada, and Australia, and isolated examples have even been reported in such far-flung places as Chile and Romania. The most popular era for this practice was the sixteenth and seventeenth centuries, when it would have been most likely done to protect the inhabitants of the buildings from the much-feared evil witches as well as their malevolent spirit familiars, but evidence suggests that the practice continued up until the early twentieth century.[28]

While it could be argued that the cats ended up in these tight spaces accidentally, getting stuck and being unable to get out again while exploring, that may only be true in some cases. It is the bizarre positioning of some of the dried, mummified bodies that indicate that they were intentionally placed after they were already dead. Dried cats are occasionally found with an equally mummified rat or mouse in a hunting-type tableau, presumably staged this way to ward off vermin. The dry and airless spaces they were entombed in would naturally mummify the corpses in the poses they were left in.

It has also been suggested that the cats could have been walled up in these small chambers while still alive, a gruesome fate for these felines, which seems unlikely as cats are known to howl quite loudly when they are unhappy, so it would take some determination—or fear of something more awful—to compel a person to do such a thing.

As the mother of modern witchcraft, Doreen Valiente, said of cats in her book *An ABC of Witchcraft Past and Present*: "The belief in occult powers associated with the cat is one of the strongest survivals of the old witch lore."[29]

---

28. Goukassian, "Another Cat in the Wall."
29. Valiente, *An ABC of Witchcraft Past & Present*, 79.

Dogs

Along with cats, it is the ever-faithful dog that tops the list of domestic pets. Dogs have lived with us for millennia, sharing our homes, food, and time as dutiful and loving pets and companions, and in some cases, they join us in the magical realms as well. And again, much like with our feline friends, it is the black-coated animals that loom large in history and folklore related to witches and the supernatural. These dogs surface throughout history and across cultures as portents of death and doom, appearing from the Underworld and disappearing into the mist without a trace, haunting lonely forests and roadways as spectres that enchant and threaten. The association of black canines with death goes back to ancient Egypt, where the jackal-headed god of death and the afterlife, Anubis, would preside over the embalming process and escort the dead to the Otherworld. The Greeks and Romans had the stories of Cerberus, the guardian of the gates of the Underworld. Norse legend tells of Garmr, a canine referred to as a dog or wolf in different sources that is related to destruction and the Underworld, which may be the same creature as Fenrir, the wolf that needed to be chained up by the gods in order to stop him from inflicting chaos and destruction across the worlds. These themes are rich in the dog folklore of Britain, where every region has its own myths and legends of black dogs with evocative names such as Black Shuck, Black Vaughn, Padfoot, Grim, or Barguest. Though the names and places change, the general description of these beasts is fairly consistent, as they are reported to be monstrously huge with shaggy black fur and glowing red eyes, sometimes wearing heavy collars or dragging chains. They are most often reported in liminal places where the veil between our world and the Underworld is thin, usually at night.

An attack by a black dog on a village church on August 4, 1577, in Bungay, Suffolk, was recorded by the Rev. Abraham Fleming in a pamphlet titled *A Strange and Terrible Wunder*. Members of the church were present for a service as a violent thunder and lightning storm lashed the community. It was then that a great black dog burst in, killing two worshippers at prayer:

> **Immediately heervpo[n] there appeared in a moste horrible similitude and likenesse to the congregation then there present a dog as they might discerne it, of a black colour: at the sight whereof, togither with the fearful flashes of fire which then were seene moved such**

admiration in the minds of the assemblie that they thought doomes day was already come. This black dog, or the divel (devil) in such a likenesse (God hee knoweth al who worketh all) runing all along the body of the Church with great swiftnesse, and incredible haste, among the people,in a visible fourm and shape, passed between two persons, as they were kneeling uppon their knees, and occupied in prayer as it seemed, wrung the necks.[30]

The folklore surrounding black dogs made it into the popular culture through the work of Sir Arthur Conan Doyle in his book *The Hound of the Baskerville*, and reports of black dog sightings are still being recorded up to this day, not only in the Dartmoor area of England where the story was set, but across the United Kingdom and North America as well.

Folklore speaks of a creature called a Puka (Irish), or Pooka, a shapeshifting being that can assume the form of a large black dog or appear in many other shapes such as that of a horse, goat, or bull; it may even appear as an attractive person. In whatever form, it still has the glowing red eyes and can also speak with a human voice. Reports of the Pooka vary by region, and the creature may be helpful or mischievous depending on where the story is from.

In 1612, the trial of the Pendle witches resulted in the hanging death of ten people, all living in the area of Pendle Hill in Lancashire, England. The trial and confessions of the accused were documented by Thomas Potts, the clerk to the Lancaster Assizes. His work stands as one of the most comprehensive accounts of a witch trial of the period. One of the accused, Alizon Device, was reported to have asked a pedlar named John Law for some pins. It is not clear if she was trying to buy them or beg some from him, but either way, he declined and continued on his way. A black dog then appeared and asked Alizon what she would like him to do to the pedlar. Alizon replied that the dog should make him lame, and within moments, the man fell to the ground, apparently lame.[31] Her confession also included details of her feeding her black dog familiar by allowing it to suckle at her breast. It was apparently her grandmother, who encouraged the relationship with the dog, who was identified in the documents

---

30. Fleming, *A Strange and Terrible Wunder*.
31. Potts, *Discovery of Witches*.

as a "devil or familiar." Alizon was found guilty of witchcraft and hanged on August 20, 1612.

Examples such as this reinforce the image of the dog, black coated or otherwise, as a favourite guise of the Devil or, at least, a favourite companion. Fearsome hounds are also featured in the lore about the Wild Hunt, a fantastic spectral cavalcade of terrifying riders on horseback, streaming across the sky or countryside. This motif is found across Norse and Germanic lands and significantly throughout Britain, France, Spain, and parts of eastern Europe. The leader of the hunt changes based on region and could be Odin, Wotan, Herne the Hunter, or Gywn ap Nudd depending on the culture and beliefs of the folk telling the story. Throughout Britain there is an association between the Hunt and the appearance of black dogs with glowing eyes and gnashing teeth, as they are said to accompany the Hunt. In Wales, however, where Gwyn ap Nudd leads, the dogs are white with blood-red ears. In many of these legends, the arrival of the Hunt is heralded by the sound of baying and barking dogs known by various names, such as Dando's Dogs, Hellhounds, Wish Hounds, or Seven Whistlers. To hear this sound was an omen of impending death and disaster.

Frogs & Toads

The lore around frogs and toads is intertwined, and it can be easy to conflate the two. Indeed, within English and European folklore the words *frog* and *toad* are often used interchangeably. It may help to remember that all toads are frogs, but not all frogs are toads, and there are a few ways to tell them apart. Both toads and frogs are amphibians belonging to the order Anura, and the differences between the two categories is largely superficial. Toads have bumpy or "warty" skin that appears dry, while frogs are smooth and appear to be wet, even when they are not in the water. Frogs have longer legs, which are designed for hopping. Toads have much shorter legs, giving them a rounder, squatter profile, and while they can hop, they tend to crawl. Frogs prefer wetlands and stick pretty close to a water source because they tend to dry out and need to be able to access the water to stay hydrated. Toad skin is tougher and better at retaining moisture, so they aren't reliant on being close to a body of water. If you see one of these creatures far from water, chances are you have a toad.

Perhaps it is the liminal nature of these creatures that captivates us. Being amphibian, they exist between land and water, deftly moving between these two worlds, swimming, hopping, or crawling with ease. In climates that experience cold winters, toads and frogs brumate, existing in another liminal space, one between waking and sleeping, life and death. Aquatic frogs will spend their brumation, a type of hibernation for cold-blooded creatures, down deep at the bottom of a lake or pond, basking on the bottom, occasionally swimming in the murk. Terrestrial toads may burrow down beneath the frost line or nestle themselves deep into an available crevice or pile of leaf litter. Some species tempt death by actually freezing solid, their bodies producing enough glucose to act as an antifreeze, protecting them from ice crystals forming in their cells. When they thaw, their organs resume function, and they apparently come back to life. Frogs that live in climates with extended dry seasons have the ability to go dormant for up to months at a time through a process called estivation. This involves the frog burrowing into the ground at the start of the dry period and shedding several layers of skin, creating a cocoon that enshrouds their entire body, leaving only their nostrils open so that they can breathe. They remain in this state until the rainy season starts, wetting the soil and signalling to the frogs that it is time to shed their cocoons and return to active life on the surface. These seemingly miraculous abilities—coupled with the ability some types of frogs and toads have to produce poisons or hallucinogens—further their reputations as liminal creatures, standing between life and death, the Middle World and the Underworld, and it is no wonder that such evocative creatures would captivate witches and magically minded folk. Toads in particular are a renowned familiar of witches. The form of a toad has been reputed to be a comfortable shape for a witch to shift into, so if you find a toad in your house, it may be best to remove it with great care as it could be a witch in disguise. Finding a toad in your house was considered unlucky in nineteenth-century Britain for this very reason, but I guess it would depend on who that witch might be and what they were up to.

Sadly for these intriguing amphibians, a large part of their historic lure has been the use of their body parts; their skin, bones, organs, and even a body part that doesn't even exist have been sought for their magical properties. Their skin and organs have been used in magical spells and healing remedies, and their bones and the mythical "toadstone" have been sought for their otherworldly powers. The toadstone was believed to be a powerful protective amulet that could detect—and also serve as an antidote to—poison. They were believed to be an effective charm against interference of fairies and demons and would be worn by mothers to protect their children from being swapped by fairies for changelings.

In order for a toadstone to work, it had to be removed from the toad while it was still alive. This was documented in the book *Lapidary, or, The History of Pretious [sic] Stones* (1652) by Thomas Nicols in which he states that "the old toad must be laid upon the cloth that is red and it will belch it up."[32] Another technique was to bury the toad in a pot in an anthill so that the ants would eat the toad, leaving behind the stone. Neither of these techniques would have been effective as the stones considered to be toadstones had nothing to do with toads or stones; they are actually the fossilized teeth of an ancient fish called a lepidote. That in itself is interesting, and how they came to be associated with this practice is unclear. However they were acquired, the "toadstone" would be worn against the skin, often set into a ring or pendant. These pieces were highly prized from the Middle Ages right to the seventeenth century, and examples of this jewelry can be seen in museums and occasionally pop up for sale at antique auctions.

> I hung the limp toad up to dry
> Overnight on a blackthorn tree, like Shecky said,
> Then stuffed it in an anthill for a month,
> And by the full moon's light pulled out a chain
> Of bones, picked clean.
> Then came the tricky part.
> You carry the skeleton to a running stream
> To ride the moonlit water, but you dare not
> Take your eyes off it till a certain bone
> Rises and floats uphill against the current;
> Then grab this bone—a little crotch bone it is,
> Shaped like a horse's hoof—and take it home,
> Bake it and break it up into a powder:
> The power's in the powder.[33]

In England, notably the East Anglia region, there is folklore about the Toadman, a person who has a supernatural ability to control horses. This power is

32. Nicols, *Lapidary*, 158–59.
33. Reibetanz, "Sam Appleby, Horseman."

gained from performing the ritual detailed in the aforementioned poem to secure a toad bone for themselves. As the poem mentions, the power is in the powder, which they must create by treating the bone with certain oils, baking it, and grinding it. The idea of frogs and toads being dried and then made into a powder comes up again and again in folk cures for any number of ailments, from sprains to cancer.

Sympathetic magic was another method that our amphibian friends would be employed in to assist with healing. The frog or toad would usually get to live through this and would be rubbed against the afflicted part of the patient with the intention that the creature would draw the problem away from the patient and into itself. There is a depiction of this in the classic 1973 film *The Wicker Man* in which the hapless Sergeant Howie enters May Morrison's shop only to find her treating a young girl for a sore throat. May coaxes the young girl into opening her mouth, saying, "It's just a little frog," neatly tucks a live frog into the girl's mouth, then removes it. May is satisfied this has worked, and she comforts the girl by assuring her the frog has her sore throat now. "Can't you hear him croaking?" she states, confident that her magic has worked.

Hares & Rabbits

The family of Leporidae consists of rabbits and hares, two categories of creatures, each with their own associations with witchcraft and magic. The differences between the two are fairly straightforward—hares are larger animals with much longer ears and legs than rabbits. Because hares tend to live out in the open, they need these long, strong appendages for running to escape predators, while rabbits will evade capture by retreating to the protection of thick bush or a burrow. A collection of burrows is a warren; it is where the rabbits of a colony live together. Hares, on the other hand, are more solitary and prefer to live alone or in pairs. Both rabbits and hares are associated with fertility, and it is no wonder as they are both prolific breeders. Hares typically will have three to four litters of two to five young, called leverets, per year, but rabbits tend to breed more frequently and have larger litters.

Along with fertility, hares and rabbits are also associated with luck, both good and bad. During the Middle Ages in Britain, it was considered very unlucky if a hare should cross your path as you set out on a journey. The same hare, or at least it's foot, would be considered a lucky charm, used to protect the bearer against various ailments and malevolent witchcraft—the same way a rabbit's foot charm would be used.

Folklore from the early modern period contains accounts of witches shape-shifting into the form of a hare, and anecdotes on this theme are found throughout Britain. One of the most famous witches of this period was Isobel Gowdie, a woman from Loch Loy in the Scottish Highlands who has become known as the Queen of Scottish Witches. She was arrested and tried for witchcraft in 1662, and it is the transcripts from her trial records that have provided us with a glimpse into the folk magic that she was accused of practising. They included her telling of various charms, including one for shapeshifting into a hare:

> **When we go into hare-shape we say:**
>
> **I shall go into a hare,**
> **With sorrow and sych (sigh) and meikel (great) care;**
> **And I shall go in the Devil's name,**
> **Aye while I come hame (home) again.**
>
> **And instantly we start into a hare. And when we want to be out of that shape, we would say:**
>
> **Hare, hare, God send thee care.**
> **I am in a hare's likeness now,**
> **But I shall be a woman even now.**[34]

It is likely that Isobel had endured some form of torture and was no doubt scared and delirious from her ordeal. The process was long; the confessions she made occurred over a six-week period and were reported in four parts. It is fascinating to read these accounts, and although Isobel would have undoubtedly been under tremendous duress, her documented words do reveal customs and beliefs that are substantiated by other recorded folklore of the time. Her words do present the opportunity to believe that she, and others with the same beliefs, could use this charm as a way to induce visions of shapeshifting in dreams or the astral plane.

---

34. Pitcairn, *Ancient Criminal Trials of Scotland*, 607.

These mysteries of the Dreamworld, of shapeshifting, and also of the moon are the realms of rabbits and hares. They are messengers and act as intermediaries, transferring information between worlds. This strong association with the mysteries of the moon, divination, and lunar deities appears in diverse cultures around the world. In Mexico, China, and Japan, for example, the "Man in the Moon" is instead a hare or rabbit. It is compelling to think that across the planet people have taken the same inspiration from the gentle actions of these creatures, interpreting their movements in our inherently human way. The image of the moongazing hare is a popular motif in contemporary Pagan art, echoing the lore of hares that sit upright on their haunches, hypnotically gazing at the moon as it rises. This may have more to do with the nocturnal nature of hares, which are most active under cover of the night. In this dreamy aspect, the connection to divination is made. Cassius Dio, a Roman historian and author of the sprawling *Histories of Rome*, tells of the revolt against the Roman Empire in Britain, led by Iceni tribal leader Boudicca in 60–61 CE.[35] He describes how Boudicca used a hare, which she had concealed within the folds of her dress, to divine the outcome of her campaign against the Roman occupiers. She released the creature and watched which way it ran. When the hare ran in the direction considered to be in the favour of the Iceni army, Boudicca raised her arms toward the heavens, thanking the lunar goddess Andraste for the positive omen. Boudicca is also said to have practiced haruspicy using the entrails of hares in attempt to divine the future of her campaign, which, in the end, was unsuccessful.

I have never seen a hare or rabbit moongaze, but I did once witness an astonishing sight as I rode a train from London to Edinburgh. As the train pulled through the rolling Scottish countryside, I was surprised to see a number of strange shapes, all apparently facing the setting sun. I had never seen hares before this and had to give my head a shake. In the few brief moments I had before the train whizzed by them, I could see that this group of hares dotting the slope along the railway line all appeared to be sitting on their haunches, watching the sunset.

---

35. Cocceianus, *The Histories of Rome*, chapter 6.

Horses

In a book by Laura Ingalls Wilder, there is a reference to a song that Laura's father sings to the family. Laura's mother disapproves of the tune, finding it too heathen for her taste.

> **The horseshoe is lucky—that's what they all say,**
> **It keeps out the spirit of wrong;**
> **It brings in the fairies at night and at day,**
> **As guardian 'tis simple but strong.**
> **When you come home at night it will keep you from fright,**
> **It brings to you blessings galore;**
> **Where'er you may dwell you will always do well,**
> **When the horseshoe hangs over the door.[36]**

As a witch, I can see that this talk of a horseshoe granting protection and bringing blessings could be construed as heathenish, and I will argue that this is a good thing.

The belief that horseshoes were lucky likely started with the belief that the iron itself was lucky, and horseshoes were a ready source of iron for those living in societies where horses were a common animal. Iron has a long folkloric history of being able to control or ward off supernatural beings, and this tale may well have its roots in the most ancient of folktales of all. The theme of the "Blacksmith and the Devil" has reappeared in folk tales reaching back to the Bronze Age,[37] morphing and adapting to the cultures and "devils" of the times and places of the people telling the stories. The basic storyline is that a cunning blacksmith tricks the Devil figure into revealing the secrets of smelting and metalworking and usually outwits the Devil in the process. This theme pops up again in Christian myth, in the story of St. Dustan, who before his sainthood was a farrier and owner of a successful forge. He was approached by the Devil himself and asked to shoe his cloven hoof. Dustan agreed to do the work but then drove a nail into a tender part of the Devil's foot and caused excruciating pain. In exchange for the nail's removal, the Devil had to promise to never

---

36. Skelly, "Keep the Horseshoe Over the Door," 97.
37. Graça and Tehrani, "Comparative Phylogenetic Analyses Uncover the Ancient Roots of Indo-European Folktales."

enter any place that displayed a horseshoe as a charm. The Devil agreed to these terms, and so now neither he nor any of his evil minions can enter any place with a protective horseshoe.

Do you hang the horseshoe open end up or down? This one is really up to you as the information on this type of charm can go both ways. I hang mine open end up, as I follow the logic that in this position the U-shaped horseshoe acts like a cup and catches and holds the good luck needed to bless the building it is mounted on and all beings that pass through the doorway that it is above. If you turn the horseshoe open end down, the luck pours out. Other folks may argue that the open side down creates a constant flowing of good luck to anyone passing underneath, so maybe it's a matter of trying both ways to see what works for you.

The skulls of horses, much like the bodies of cats, have been concealed in buildings as a form of protection. Horses were believed to be sensitive and vulnerable to the malevolent work of witches and fairies, and the concealed horse skull would act as bait, drawing the evil influence away from the inhabitants of the building and to the skull. The folk belief that horses were susceptible to magical attack may have been the inspiration for attaching decorative horse brasses, which often have symbolic shapes, to their bridals and straps, the idea being that the shiny metal of the ornaments was effective at warding off the evil eye or witchcraft.

It may not always be practical to wear or carry an actual horseshoe around with you, but incorporating the symbol of one is easy enough to do. Traditionally a horseshoe is fixed to the hoof using seven nails—seven being a number associated with luck fairly universally. By incorporating the symbol of the horseshoe shape, the number seven, and the belief that the horseshoe can provide luck and safety from evil spirits, you can use this symbol to do many different types of protective and prosperity magic.

Moles

Moles are small humble animals that were among the creatures considered to be a familiar animal of witches, and a description of one case can be found in the trial record of Joan Willimott, a woman who, in 1618, admitted to practicing witchcraft and keeping the company of a familiar. Joan's case is interesting as she freely admitted to these charges and argued that her witchcraft was benevolent and that her familiar spirit was only concerned with healing. Joan was accused of consorting with a moliwarp, or mole, and also a kitten, both of which she fed by allowing them to suck at her neck—one on the right side, the other on the left.[38] Joan, her moliwarp, and the kitten got off easy and were released, escaping execution.

Moles, or at least their body parts, were also popular as charms for healing. This didn't work out so well for the poor moles, as most of the charms and techniques that involved them required the moles to be killed, usually in a gruesome and cruel way. Cutting one or more feet off of a mole and placing them in a pouch to be worn around the neck was thought to cure epilepsy and toothache. The mutilated and still-living mole would be released to crawl away and die slowly, the idea being that it would take the health problem away with it. A cure for rheumatism also called for mole paws to be cut off and carried around in the pockets of the patient. Another epilepsy cure involved slitting the throat of a live mole and draining its blood into a glass of wine that was to be drunk by the afflicted person. This connection between moles and healing also led to a belief that if you held a mole in your hand until it died, the healing power of the mole would transfer into the hand of the holder, granting them the power of healing.

Owls

Beloved of many contemporary witches, owls have been associated with deities, myth, and folklore from a wide array of cultures. Witches and owls are linked in the folklore of multiple cultures and throughout history.

Being mostly nocturnal creatures, their ghostly movements at night align them with the moonlit world of dreams, psychic ability, intuition, and spirit. There is some British folklore surrounding owls, but most of the truly fascinating mythology connecting owls to witches comes from antiquity, starting with the Jewish folklore of Lilith, said to be the first wife of Adam. She left the Garden of Eden to pursue her own destiny and is thought to be the first witch, able to shapeshift into animal form, becoming a snake, black cat, or an owl. One of the theories surrounding a piece of Sumerian art, a terra cotta plaque dated to 2300 BCE called the Burney Relief, is that it is a depiction of Lilith. The female figure has bird wings and feet, and it was flanked on both sides by large owls. In the ancient Greek world, owls held a very high status due to their association

---

38. *The Wonderful Discoverie of the Witchcrafts of Margaret and Phillip Flower.*

with the goddess Athena, and to see one was thought to be an indication of her favour. Minerva, the Roman equivalent of Athena, also had the owl as her emblem, representing wisdom, which is an association that is embedded in owl lore wherever they are found.

The strix was another zoomorphic creature with the body of an owl and the head of a woman. The literal translation of *strix* is "screech owl," and it did indeed possess a screech that would strike fear and was believed to be a harbinger of war and disaster. Ancient Romans believed the strigae (plural form) to be female witches who would take owl form in order to fly by night, feed on human flesh, and steal newborn babies. Strigae may appear human during the day, but by night they would reveal themselves in beast form, out to fulfill their sexual appetites and other nefarious acts. Not unlike Lilith, the strigae were fearsome, powerful, and liberated females that upset the status quo of the time.

The Welsh story cycle, the Mabinogion, includes a story about Blodeuwedd, a beautiful woman formed out of flowers to serve as wife to Llew Llaw Gyffes, son of Arianrhod. When Blodeuwedd betrays Llew, she is turned into an owl. As a goddess, she could not be put to death for her actions, so instead she was condemned to spend eternity hunting by night, taking a form that implies she is in league with the dark forces of nature, as punishment for her actions against Llew.

Common folklore from across Britain warns that an owl knocking at your window is a very bad omen, as is hearing the sound of a barn owl screeching. Catching sight of an owl flying by day is interpreted as a portent of doom and disaster. In the Middle Ages, the hooting sound of an owl was a sign that a witch was nearby. A folk charm for improving eyesight involved cooking an owl egg down to ash, then incorporating it into a potion and consuming it.

Ravens & Crows

These characterful corvids are a perennial favourite of witches, to be sure. This may be due to their beauty, intelligence, and associations with gods and goddesses, which really resonate with modern witchcraft practitioners. Both ravens and crows are resourceful animals that are capable of imitating human speech, a talent that has no doubt contributed to their reputations as tricksters and messengers of the gods. Both crows and ravens are known as carrion eaters, feeding on already dead and decomposing bodies of people and animals, which leads them to being associated with deities of warfare and death, flying over battlefields looking for an easy meal in the chaos of war and destruction. In fact, these birds are opportunistic eaters, hunting, foraging, and taking advantage of carrion as they find it. The role of these great black birds as psychopomps, carrying the souls of the dead to the next world, is no doubt linked to the observation of them picking over the bones of the dead. These corvids also have death rituals of their own and will hold "funerals" when one of their own is found dead. A crow, for instance, will call out an alarm when it finds another crow dead, signalling to crows in the area to attend. The birds then form a big noisy group that caws and makes a disturbance for about fifteen to twenty minutes before gradually dispersing. It is one thing to read about this, but when I witnessed this actually happening in my neighbourhood, I was astounded by how many crows showed up to mourn a dead crow that was laying on the road a block from my house. Dozens of birds swooped in, and the noise was deafening. I left my home office to see what the ruckus was, and it was an amazing sight, lasting for about half an hour from the first noisy outburst to the last crow leaving.

Folklore generally considers ravens and crows to be harbingers of bad luck and misfortune. One spotted alone—or even the sound of one's call—is considered an omen of death. Two of them sighted together could be considered good luck, and a group of three is a clear message that change is imminent. The collective nouns for these birds also carry negative connotations—a group of crows is called a "murder" and a group of ravens is an "unkindness." Not the best publicity for these clever birds.

Even the British monarchy is susceptible to the lure of ravens and maintains a number of them within the Tower of London. According to legend, if the ravens ever leave the Tower, the kingdom will fall. In order to ensure that this would never happen, King Charles II, while ruling in the 1600s, decreed that ravens must be kept at the Tower and protected. This tradition continues to this day, and the birds have a specially appointed staff and Raven Master who attend to their needs. Further back in the mythic history of Britain, the legendary King Arthur, according to a story from Cornwall, transformed into a raven and lives on in the body of the bird. As a result of this, killing ravens is taboo in that part of the country—"just in case." In Wales, folklore states that a raven cawing from a steeple overlooking a house indicates that a member of the household will soon die. A Scottish legend is that feeding a small child a drink from the skull of a raven will grant them second sight.

Snakes

Snakes rise from our collective unconscious evoking conflicting images. They are associated with hidden wisdom, sacred mysteries, oracular messages, death, and destruction, but they also represent the constructive forces of birth, rebirth, creation, healing, and fertility. The image of the ouroboros, the snake that has curled back onto itself, forming a circle and swallowing its own tail, illustrates the never-ending cycle of death and rebirth, creation and destruction. As the snake sheds its skin, it emerges from its former self reborn, shiny and renewed. The ouroboros can represent reproductive union, the tail being the penetrative partner and the mouth being the receptive partner. The cycles of the snake are the cycles of witchcraft, honouring the tides of nature.

The associations these serpents have with the darker side of nature come from human fear of the Underworld, death, and darkness—all things that snakes can navigate fluently. When the snake was cast as the villain in the Garden of Eden, it came to represent our repressed desires and fears, which earned it the wrath of God and his followers.

Folklore from England tells of adders that were believed to be able to swallow their young if danger was near and then spit them back out when the threat was gone. This echoes the old wives' tale that you must always sleep with your mouth closed lest a snake slither into your mouth. I just can't imagine a snake thinking this was a good idea. In rural Australia and also England, it was believed that even if you kill a snake during the day, it won't actually die until after the sun sets. It is interesting that there is a pattern of stories from all over the world of giant snakes that swallow the sun or moon, causing eclipses. There are also stories that cross the globe of snakes that drink wine, suckle milk from nursing mothers or livestock, and crave blood to drink.[39] These stories are part of a folkloric sub-genre that includes stories of a number of types of animals that feed off of the bosom of women or raid cattle sheds to feed on milk. These tales say more about the fears and phobias of the storytellers and are more bad press for the snakes, as snakes do not possess the anatomy to latch on and suckle, or process lactose, nor are they known in reality to seek out wine or blood.

Snakes have a long history with healing as well and are famously depicted coiled around the rod of Asclepius, the ancient Greek god of medicine and

---

39. Ermacora, "The Comparative Milk-Sucking Reptile."

healing, who learned the healing arts from a serpent that whispered the secrets to him. The ability that snakes have to brumate deep in the ground, in a dormant, deathlike state, then return to the surface, alive and well, going on to shed their skin and appear healthy and refreshed, reinforces the snake's connection to healing and vitality.

Other Animals Found in Witchcraft

All animals, from the smallest insect to the largest whale, can have magical associations. As modern witches, many of us form connections with creatures that live beyond our own bioregions, and they may be animals that we have never even seen in real life. Animals from different parts of the world may have associations and correspondences that are helpful to our own magic, so here, for reference, is a list of some common animals with some of their associated key words

Bears	Birth, hibernation, grounding, confidence, healing
Butterflies	Transformation, metamorphosis, change, vitality, purity
Coyotes	Resourceful, trickster, humour, fun, mischief
Deer	Harmony, sexuality, protection, sacrifice, sensitivity
Dolphins	Communication, compassion, playful, energy, intuition
Eagles	Leadership, freedom, spirit, knowledge, longevity
Foxes	Observation, diplomacy, cunning, creativity, discretion
Goats	Stubborn, determination, fertility, stamina, libido
Hawks	Vigilance, perspective, omens, observation, defence
Ladybugs	Luck, fortune, happiness, abundance, trust
Lions	Dignity, loyalty, authority, valour, royalty
Mice	Details, organization, instinct, opportunism, gentleness
Peacocks	Beauty, divinity, pride, luxury, masculinity,
Pigs	Protection, luck, abundance, excess, wealth

Rats	Repression, adaptability, envy, resourcefulness, procreation
Salmon	Journey, development, knowledge, wisdom, nourishment
Spiders	Fate, possibility, consciousness, communication, messages
Turtles	Earth, steadiness, old age, home, retreat,
Vultures	Death, exhaustion, rebirth, renewal, self-reliance
Weasels	Solitary, tenacious, analytical, ingenuity, stealth
Whales	Contemplation, telepathy, truth, communication, solitude
Wolves	Leadership, structure, community, family, learning

From Folklore to Practice

In reading the strange, wonderful, and fantastic folklore surrounding animals, we can see that times have certainly changed and our attitudes and beliefs about animals have too. Science has expanded our understanding of how the world works, and we no longer allow superstition to dictate our behaviour toward things we do not understand … well, most of the time, anyway.

What we can take from these folkloric examples is that there is an undeniable bond between witches and animals and that those animals can be actual physical animals or animals in spirit form. This presents us with a challenge. Can we allow ourselves to believe that encoded in these folktales, myths, legends, and superstitions there are slivers of truth and repeating patterns of wisdom? Perhaps if we distill these kernels of truth, we can weave them together and tease out knowledge of a deeper magic that we can work with the aid of animals.

CHAPTER FOUR
Companions of the Gods

The realm of the gods is equally inhabited by animals, creatures that assist and serve their deities, embodying the attributes and archetypes of their divine counterparts. In some examples, the deity may be zoomorphic, possessing the features of the animal, and in other cases, the deity may have the animal as a mascot or emblem. However they appear together, this pattern of deities and animals appears in every corner of the globe, across cultures and religious beliefs. As witches, we may choose to involve the presence of gods or goddesses in our practice as guardians, as patrons, or to provide inspiration. They may be petitioned for favours, or we may perform devotional work to them, and this may be in part due to the animals they are associated with. In my own experience, I was drawn to Roman goddess Diana more for her association with dogs than for her association with witchcraft. Seeing her represented in art surrounded by nature with her dogs beside her is so relatable to my own life and how I experience the sacred, walking with my dogs in wild places and experiencing the mystery and beauty of the natural world together.

In the Hindu tradition, animals appear as a god's *vahana*, or vehicle, providing a means of transportation for the deity to travel from the Upper World, in which they live, to other realms. The vahana are given as much honour and respect as the gods themselves by devotees who give offerings and prayers to the sacred creatures. The vahana have distinct personalities and can appear on their own, being regarded as a partner in the divine work of the god they are associated with. Greek gods also have animals to guide their travels and are depicted driving chariots being drawn by their sacred animals. Helios had his white, winged horses, Demeter was pulled by serpents, and Hera had her peacocks to power her travel, to name a few.

In ancient Egyptian religion, gods took on the physical characteristics of animals that could express their qualities or their disposition. Sekhmet, for example, is the lion-headed goddess of pestilence, destruction, and war but also healing. Her name translates to "powerful one," and she is loved and revered for her fearlessness and ferocity in battle, which is balanced by her loyalty and tenderness in her healing aspect. This profile fits the symbolism of the lioness, an animal that embodies the same characteristics throughout time of being a fierce fighter and tender mother to her cubs.

Animal features or animal companions assert the personality, attributes, and powers of the deities. The animal becomes an extension of that god's or goddess's being, and the deity is made greater and also more relatable by the animal's contribution. Throughout time, devotees have donned animal skins or masks to imitate animals, and so honour both the gods and the animals. It is a relatively recent invention that humans have dominion over animals and have rejected them as our allies, our relatives, our kin. Historically, humans have elevated the creatures native to their environment into the world of gods and spirits, the animals being seen as life givers and divine in their own right. Over time we have generally forgotten this, and the respect we should have for our animal family has dissipated. Particularly in the West, we are less and less connected to the world of animals, and their relationship to us is no longer as valued as it was when we needed them for food, shelter, and clothing. Mainstream society is also less inclined to relate to gods and goddesses as well, for that matter. But for witches, who can see the value in maintaining and growing these relationships, with gods and animals, there is real potential for wisdom and fulfillment.

It is not essential to work with deities in order to practice witchcraft, but many of us do hear the call of a deity, or several deities, and work with them in one way or another. The god or goddess that resonates with us may be a conscious choice, made after careful consideration and research, or it may be the result of feeling that "tap on the shoulder" from a deity that has singled you out. Traditions and individual covens may have a patron deity that the members honour together, or they may be chosen on a seasonal or occasional basis. There is no one right way to decide these things, and that is one of the great things about witchcraft. It is a craft, and practice makes perfect. You get to choose whom you feel called to honour, worship, or work with.

The animals associated with a god or goddess is a contributing factor in choosing which deity will suit the magic at hand. I feel an affinity for Hecate, goddess of witchcraft who is known for her close bond with dogs. This is very easy for me to relate to, my own dogs being my closest companions. I have also made donations to cat shelters in the name of Bast, a goddess who appears in cat form and is a protector of women and children. My witchcraft includes devotional work for the Horned God, and his emblematic animal, the stag, is forever with me.

This chapter offers a short guide to animals and the deities that they are related to. A complete listing would be a gigantic tome, so this brief list is a starting point.

Bat

Camazotz (Mayan)—This fearsome god has the head of a bat and the body of a human man. His origin appears to be from the region of Oaxaca, Mexico, in and around 100 BCE. His notoriety spread throughout Mesoamerica. His name comes from the K'iche people of Guatemala and translates to "death bat." He is, not surprisingly, associated with death and the Underworld.

Bear

Artemis (Greek)—As a goddess of nature, hunting, and women's mysteries, Artemis is associated with a few animals, the bear being an important one. The bear was a symbol for a rite of passage festival, the *arkteia*, which was held at Brauron in ancient Greece to mark a girl's transition into womanhood. A legend of the region tells of a young girl provoking and then being scratched by a tamed she-bear in a shrine of Artemis. The bear was killed by the girl's brothers in retaliation. This so angered Artemis that a famine ensued. She exerts a "mother bear" protectiveness over young animals and humans, particularly young, athletic, and warrior woman. Artemis came to be identified with the Roman goddess Diana.

Artio (Celtic)—The name of this goddess translates to "bear," and she is a guardian of bears and other wild animals. A statue found near Bern, Switzerland, in 1832 shows Artio in bear form as well as human form along with a bowl of fruit, signifying abundance. It is inscribed with the words "for the goddess Artio, from

Licinia Sabinilla" and is dated to about the second or third century CE. Bear cults were popular throughout not only Switzerland but through what is now France, western Germany, northern Italy, and parts of Belgium. Artio is closely associated with the Greek Artemis and the Roman Diana.

Bee

Aristaios (Greek)—Considered a minor god of the Greek pantheon, Aristaios was the god of bee-related things, such as beekeeping, honey, and mead, as well as cheese making, olive oil, herbs, and hunting. He was beloved of shepherds and rural folk. Some stories tell of him starting out as human, but he then ascended to the role of a god thanks to the gifts he gave humankind. The root of his name comes from *aristos*, which translates to either "most useful" or "most excellent."

Ra (Egyptian)—Archeological evidence supports a theory that the first people to practice beekeeping were Egyptians during the Bronze Age, around 3100 BCE. According to legend the first bees fell to earth as the tears of the sun god Ra and that the bees bore his sacred messages to humankind.

Bull

Apis (Egyptian)—Apis was an ancient god in the form of a bull who was honoured in Egypt as early as 3150–2890 BCE. He began as a fertility god of grain crops and animal herds and over time went on to become connected with the Underworld as he became associated with deities such as Osiris, Otah, and Sokaris. In Egypt he is often depicted as having a solar disc between his horns and is sometimes considered the son of Hathor and shares her associations with abundance and benevolence.

Dionysus (Greek)—As a god of wine, ecstasy, and wild frenzy, Dionysus has strong associations with the earthy pleasures of sexuality, intoxication, sensual indulgence, and male potency. He is believed to manifest as a bull, and these creatures were often used as sacrifices to him. In Orphic Hymn 44 to Dionysus, he is evoked with: "Come, blessed Dionysus, various-named, bull-faced, begot from thunder, Bacchus famed." In Hymn 29, the bull theme is repeated as: "Rural, ineffable, two-formed, obscure, two-horned, with ivy crowned, and

Euion pure: bull-faced and martial, bearer of the vine, endued with counsel prudent and divine."[40]

Indeed, the symbol of the bull for the earthy, potent, and virile exploits of Dionysus is understandable.

Zeus (Greek)—This god is associated with multiple animals, but it was the form of a white bull that Zeus shifted into in order to evade his wife, Hera, and get close to the exquisitely beautiful young woman Europa. The white bull so transfixed her that she climbed up on his back. Zeus seized this opportunity and immediately ran for the sea and swam to Crete, where he revealed his true form and raped Europa. She eventually bore him three sons, and she became the namesake of the continent of Europe. Zeus came to be identified with the Roman god Jupiter.

Butterfly

Itzpapalotl (Aztec)—Itzpapalotl is a fearsome warrior goddess who rules over Tamoanchan, a paradise for women and babies who have died in childbirth. Her name translates to "obsidian butterfly" or "clawed butterfly," as she has beautiful dark wings and fierce talons. She is a sorceress who protects women and children and is a guardian of the crossroads.

Cat

Freya (Norse)—She is the goddess of sex, death, fertility, war, love, and the pre-Christian form of Norse witchcraft known as *seidr*. It comes as no surprise that where there is witchcraft, there will be cats. Freya's mode of transportation is a chariot drawn by a pair of cats who are reputed to be domestic felines, gray or sometimes blue in colour.

Bast/Bastet (Egyptian)—Another of the zoomorphic deities, Bast is depicted as either a cat or as a shapely woman with a cat's head. Like Freya she has an association with magic and also with sex, fertility, pregnancy, healing, and prosperity. In her earliest recorded manifestations, she was regarded as fierce. Over time her image softened, and the aggressive traits were transposed onto the goddess

---

40. Taylor, *The Hymns of Orpheus.*

Sekhmet, who was seen as wrathful as opposed to the protective qualities of the "domesticated" feline nature of Bast.

Cheetah

Mafdet (Egyptian)—The earliest of the recorded feline goddesses, Mafdet, or Mefdet, had the head of a cheetah or sometimes a cat, lynx, or leopard. She was a goddess of legal judgement and capital punishment, dispatching quick and fatal sentences to the accused. She offered protection from snakes and venomous creatures.

Cow

Hathor (Egyptian)—A goddess of love, birth, fertility, and drunkenness, Hathor is represented in ancient art as a beautiful woman, sometimes with cow ears or horns, or as a cow with a solar disc between her horns. As a matron goddess of women, she was called the Mother of Mothers and presided over the reproductive roles of women, and as the Celestial Nurse, she presided over the heavens, the Milky Way pouring from her breasts.

Dodola (Slavic)—Sometimes referred to as Perperuna, she flies over the land in the springtime, covering the land with lush greenery and flowers. She is associated with rain, which she creates by "milking" her cows, the clouds. If she is accompanied by her husband, Perun, the god of thunder, she co-creates storms.

Crocodile

Sobek (Egyptian)—Sobek is a god of the Nile River, appearing with the body of a man and the head of a crocodile or entirely as a crocodile. He represents the fertility and abundance that the Nile River brought to the land. The strength, speed, and ferocity of the crocodile side of his nature made Sobek the patron of armies and protector of the pharaohs.

Deer

Diana (Roman)—A goddess of the wild places, hunting, and animals, Diana is strongly associated with witchcraft. As Diana Venetrix, the goddess of the hunt, she is commonly depicted carrying a bow and arrow, wearing a short hunting-style tunic, and accompanied by deer, one of her sacred animals. Diana came to be identified with the Greek goddess Artemis.

Cernunnos (Celtic)—Historic accounts of this deity are rare; all that we have are images of him depicted as a human male with the antlers of a stag, usually wearing a torc around his neck, and surrounded by animals. Despite the scarcity of lore, he is adored by modern witches and Pagans as the Horned One, Lord of the Wild Places, and Lord of Death and Resurrection.

Dog

Cunomaglus (Celtic)—Cunomaglus is an elusive and little-known god from the Cotswolds region of Britain. An inscription describes him as the "Great Hound Lord," and he is thought to be a god of hunting. He was later conflated with the Roman god Apollo.

Diana (Roman)—As a goddess of the hunt, Diana is seen with her hunting dogs by her side. She presides over witchcraft, magic, fertility, and childbirth. She is a protector of the oppressed, outlaws, and slaves. She is identified with the Greek goddess Artemis and shares the story of Actaion spying on her only to be destroyed by her loyal hounds. She is also associated with deer and wolves.

Gwyn ap Nudd (Welsh)—In Welsh myth, Gwynn ap Nudd is the ruler of the Underworld who leads the Wild Hunt, a ghostly collection of dead warriors who race across the sky. The spectral procession is accompanied by Cwn Annwn, the spectral hounds that help the Hunt gather the souls of the dead. To hear the sound of these hounds baying is a portend of death.

Hecate (Greek)—Beloved goddess of the crossroads, witchcraft, and the night, Hecate is seldom without the company of her dogs, her most sacred animal. Dogs were offered as sacrifice to her in ancient times in ceremonies held at the new moon. Dogs were seen to be guardians of the Underworld as they were observed scavenging in graveyards, another liminal place associated with Hecate. She can be called upon when doing magic for the protection of her beloved canines.

Dolphin

Poseidon (Greek)—When Poseidon fell in love with the beautiful Amphitrite, he called on dolphins to help him. Amphitrite fled from Poseidon and tried to hide on the other side of the earth. The dolphins were sent to find her and persuaded her to accept Poseidon's love. To show his gratitude, Poseidon set the dolphin in the sky as the constellation Delphinus. Poseidon came to be identified with the Roman god Neptune.

Donkey

Hephaestus (Greek)—This blacksmith god, the Limping One, was either born lame or became lame after being cast out into the sea by his mother, Hera, for being ugly. This disability may be why he is shown often in Greek art riding on a donkey. This choice of mount is interesting because typically the Greek deities are known to ride chariots. The donkey implies a more humble and industrial personality. Known as Vulcan to the Romans, he is a god of fire, blacksmithing, metalwork, sculpture, and stonemasonry.

Dove

Aphrodite (Greek)—This goddess of love, fertility, and beauty has a golden, jewel-encrusted cart that is drawn by a team of doves, beautiful birds that are associated with love as well as peace and loyalty. In some myths, Aphrodite, or Venus, to the Romans, was born from an egg incubated by doves.

Eagle

Zeus (Greek)—The eagle was the companion and messenger of Zeus, or Jupiter, as he was known to the Romans. This great bird accompanied and assisted Zeus on many adventures. It kidnapped the young Trojan prince Ganymede for Zeus, carrying him off to Mount Olympus to serve as Zeus's cupbearer. The eagle dealt out Zeus's punishment to Prometheus for giving fire to humans, eating his liver every day only to have it grow back at night so the eagle could eat it again the next day. The constellation Aquila is said to be Zeus's loyal eagle.

Perun (Slavic)—The chief of the Slavic gods, Perun is master of thunder, justice, and war. He was honoured widely across eastern Europe despite the regional differences in customs and myths of the numerous Slavic tribes. His sacred tree is the oak, representing the World Tree, and Perun would shapeshift into the form of an eagle and sit atop it.

Falcon

Freya (Norse)—Known for her disposition toward the finer things in life, Freya enjoyed her material possessions. Her cat-drawn chariot, prized amber necklace, and magical cloak made of falcon feathers were her most famous. The falcon cloak gave her, or anyone she would loan it to, the ability to fly. The feathers were also said to have granted her the ability shapeshift into falcon form. She is also associated with other animals, including cats, rabbits, and boars.

Horus (Egyptian)—A god of the sun and sky, Horus has the body of a man and the head of a falcon or is entirely a falcon with magnificent wings. His left eye represented the moon and his right eye the sun while his wings were the sky. His epithets include Horus of Two Horizons, Horus the Lord of the Sky, and Horus the Sky God. His worship spanned such a great length of time and was later adopted by the Greeks, creating a long, confusing story that spans many archetypes and manifestations.

Fish

Danu (Celtic)—The Great Mother of Ireland, Danu is also "the flowing one" associated with earth, fertility, and water in the form of flowing rivers, oceans, and springs. Fish, particularly salmon, are related to her.

Fox

Inari (Japanese)—This deity appears as male, female, or androgynous, with different manifestations carrying different correspondences. Inari is the deity, or *kami*, of a host of things including agriculture (rice in particular), fertility, tea, abundance, and success in industry. The fox spirit, *kitsune*, is Inari's close ally, acting as a protector, messenger, or sometimes mount. The kitsune are spirits known for being wily and extremely clever, and although kitsune are supernatural beings, any fox may be a messenger to Inari, so it is expected that all foxes be treated with kindness and respect.

Goat

Pan (Greek)—This beloved god of nature has the upper body of a man and the tail, shaggy legs, and cloven hoofs of a goat. He is the god of shepherds and their flocks, lust, ecstasy, music, and the wild, free, and primal aspects of human nature. His sexual exploits are legendary as he freely pursued whomever he pleased, including the goats he roamed the wilds of Arcadia with. Pan was depicted in ancient art as very rustic, often with an erect phallus, playing his panpipe and occasionally in flagrante delicto with a she-goat. As time passed, his image was tamed down, and he became more human. Pan came to be identified with the Roman god Faunus.

Thor (Norse)—Riding his chariot drawn by Tanngrisnir and Tanngnjóstr, both goats, Thor is a mighty warrior and god of thunder, which rolls from the wheels as he travels with his cloven-hoofed companions. The trust between Thor and the goats was deep. Thor could sacrifice Tanngrisnir and Tanngnjóstr when food was needed, and their meat could be consumed as long as none of their bones were broken. Thor could then resurrect them by swinging his great hammer, Mjölnir.

Hare/Rabbit

Andraste (Celtic)—This lunar goddess of war and victory is also associated with divination. She is remembered in the writings of the Roman historian Dio Cassius, who wrote an account of the revolt led by British Iceni tribal queen Boudicca against Roman invaders is 60 CE. According to Cassius, Boudicca believed that the outcome of her campaign against Rome could be determined by the movements of a hare. Upon invoking the goddess, Boudicca released a hare from the folds of her dress to see which way it would run. The hare took off in a direction that appeared to be in Boudicca's favour. Boudicca then thanked Andraste for this omen and embarked on her fearsome attack against the Roman army, burning Roman settlements as her army advanced.

Kaltes (Siberian)—Sacred to the Urgic people of Western Siberia and sometimes referred to as Kaltes-Ekwa, she is a lunar goddess who presides over fertility, childbirth, fate, and rejuvenation. She is a shapeshifter, known to assume the form of a hare or rabbit, animals known for their own fertile and prolific habits and moon associations.

Hawk

Nephthys (Egyptian)—Daughter of Geb and Nut and sister of Isis, Nephthys is a goddess of magic, death, darkness, immortality, and beer. Professional mourners were sometimes employed for Egyptian funerals and were known as Hawks of Nephthys. Her association with mortuaries and embalming was inherited by her son, Anubis.

Hen

Hebe (Greek)—Daughter of Hera and Zeus, Hebe is a goddess of youth, beauty, and brides. Hebe was considered as beautiful as her mother and served as a cupbearer to the Olympians, serving them sweet nectar and ambrosia. She was married to the hero Hercules after he ascended as a god to Mount Olympus. In ancient times, hens were kept in a sacred temple to Hebe and were fed and cared for in her honour, while cocks were kept in the adjoining temple to Hercules, the two kept separate by a stream of flowing water.

Hippopotamus

Taweret (Egyptian)—A primarily protective goddess, Taweret has the body of a hippo and stands tall on her hind legs. Her image was made into the forms of amulets that would be used for apotropaic purposes and to protect mothers and babies from the dangers of childbirth and childhood illnesses.

Horse

Epona (Celtic)—The worship of Epona, the Great Mare, patron goddess of horses and foals, was widespread across Celtics lands, and her influence was so potent that it was adopted by the Romans, whose cavalry took her with them back to Rome. She is seen as a single woman, surrounded by horses, and bearing a cornucopia to symbolize abundance and fertility. She is also linked to sovereignty and the divine connection between leadership and the land.

Shango (Yoruban)—Potent and beautiful, exuding courage and vitality, Shango, the orisha of thunder and lightning, rides a horse as a sign of his power, as these animals were status symbols for kings and warriors. In some stories, he rides a white horse named Eshinla, and in others, he rides a black horse and it is said that an effigy of such a horse should be placed in his shrines.

Jackal

Anubis (Egyptian)—The towering and forbidding form of Anubis, the all-black, jackal-headed god of the afterlife and mummification, is one of the oldest in the Egyptian pantheon. His dark black body symbolizes decay and regeneration. He is the protector and escort of the dead as they enter the Hall of Judgement and is depicted on the walls of tombs attending to the mummification of corpses, presiding over funerals, or weighing the heart of a soul against the white feather of truth.

Wepwawet (Egyptian)—Predating Anubis, Wepwawet is a jackal-headed or sometimes wolf-headed deity often associated with death and the Underworld. His name translates to "the opener of the ways," and this refers to the "roads" we face in our lives and afterlives—birth, life, and death—and roads to success and prosperity and opportunity.

Lion

Nergal (Sumerian)—An ancient god of destruction, pestilence, and death, Nergal personifies the forces of nature that destroy without judgement or remorse, but simply because it is part of nature that things must be destroyed. He wields a mace that is topped with two lion heads, and he also appears in the form of a winged lion, the animal being associated with the same fearless and ferocious characteristics as the god himself.

Sekhmet (Egyptian)—The fearsome and intimidating Sekhmet has the head of a female lion, crowned with a solar disc, and the body of a woman. She is credited with creating the desert from her breath. Her fearless lioness aspect is celebrated as a vengeful goddess of war and destruction, but in her softer feline form, she is revered as an adept healer and matron of doctors.

Monkey

Hanuman (Hindu)—Monkey-faced god of compassion, intelligence, devotion, and strength, Hanuman was mischievous child with an insatiable appetite. When he mistook the sun for a ripe mango, he jumped into the sky to eat it, enraging the god Indra, who struck him with a thunderbolt, breaking his jaw. This is how he got his name, which translates to "disfigured jaw." Hanuman's mother was the goddess Anjani, who was transformed into a monkey by Pavarti for allegedly flirting with her husband, Shiva.

Owl

Athena (Greek)—Also known as Minerva to the Romans, Athena is a virgin warrior goddess depicted in full armor, often carrying a helmet and spear. She rules over war and peace, creativity and intelligence, and she was renowned for her creative and inventive abilities. The owl, also being a creature of intelligence and superior hunting ability, is her ally and symbol.

Blodeuwedd (Welsh)—She arose from the stories of the Mabinogion as a beautiful maiden, created out of flowers to serve as a bride for Lleu, as he was cursed to never be able to marry a mortal woman. When Blodeuwedd fell in love with another man, she conspired to kill Lleu and was thwarted by the wizard Gwydion, who turned her into an owl. Her name translates alternately to "flower face" or "owl."

Lakshmi (Hindu)—In India, the owl is a bird that represents wisdom and intelligence, its large round eyes imparting a sense of focus. Lakshmi is a goddess of prosperity, wealth, and health, and the owl's virtues are thought to compliment the Lakshmi's attributes. The owl serves as Lakshmi's vahana, or mount, and she is often depicted riding the owl's back or with the owl seated at her feet.

Panther

Dionysus (Greek)—Dionysus is the Olympian god of ecstasy, intoxication, madness, wine, and pleasure, and worship of Dionysus includes the pleasures of the flesh, such as music, revelry, and orgiastic indulgence. He is depicted in art from antiquity holding his drinking cup and his rather phallic pinecone-tipped staff while mounted on the back of a panther. Being an earthy, rustic deity, he is related to many animals, including goats, lions, bulls, and serpents.

Peacock

Hera (Greek)—The wife of Zeus, a god well known for his infidelities, Hera became angry when he began an affair with Io, his latest mistress. She recruited Argus to watch over Io with his hundred eyes. Enraged, Zeus sent Hermes to slay Argus, and when Hera learned of his death, she took Argus's hundred eyes and set them on the tail of a peacock in honour of his memory. She came to love these birds so much that she had them pull her chariot. Hera came to be identified with the Roman goddess Juno.

Pig

Hestia (Greek)—The humble and gentle Hestia is a goddess of hearth and home. She is equated with the Roman goddess Vesta. Her duties include overseeing the preparation of food and tending the flames where ritual sacrifice would be accepted. It was said that Hestia would feed the ritual fire on Mount Olympus with pig fat to keep it burning bright. The pig was also the animal of choice for making sacrificial offerings to Hestia, as it is a domestic animal that shares many of her gentle and generous attributes.

Ram

Hermes (Greek)—One of the original twelve gods of Olympus, Hermes presides over language, astronomy, roads, and diplomacy. These attributes are fitting as he also served as personal messenger for Zeus, the leader of the Olympians. There are many depictions of Hermes riding on the back of a giant ram, which reflects his role as a god of herds and flocks. Hermes came to be identified with the Roman god Mercury.

Raven/Crow

Morrígan (Irish)—A fearsome and awesome goddess of war, sex, death, and sovereignty, Morrígan's bird is the raven or crow, both birds being carrion eaters that will pick over the bodies of those slain in combat. She is a shapeshifter, appearing in her feathered form as an omen of death on the battlefield. The shriek of the Morrígan is like that of the banshee, bringing death to those who hear it. This is echoed less fatally in the caw of the crow or the gronk of the raven.

Odin (Norse)—Equally the god of poetry and war, Odin, the All-father, is the ruler and chief of the *Aesir*, the principal pantheon of Norse gods. Odin relies on the keen intelligence of his raven companions, Hugin and Munin, who journey far and wide on behalf of Odin, either as avian informers or as projections of aspects of Odin himself, on the quest for wisdom and knowledge.

Scarab (Dung Beetle)

Khepri (Egyptian)—His name translates as "to come into being" or "to emerge." This reflects the belief that it was he who pushed the sun across the sky throughout the day and then down into the Underworld at night, much like how the scarab beetle would push balls of dung down into its burrow. Although no temples or shrines to Khepri have been discovered, the scarab was an important and popular motif for jewelry, art, funerary adornment, and domestic decoration. They represent protection, good luck, spiritual power, and rebirth and are still a popular talismanic item to this day.

Sheep

Mokosh (Slavic)—Considered to be a mother goddess, Mokosh is a bringer of fertility with power over earth and water. Bearing a spindle, she is the guardian of sheep and shepherds, the spinning of wool and weaving of threads.

Snake

Apep (Egyptian)—Also known as Apophis, Apep is an ancient spirit of chaos, evil, and destruction in the form of a snake.

Asclepius (Greek)—The most recognizable symbol of Asclepius is the rod of Asclepius, which features a snake twining around a staff. This potent symbol has come to represent the medical profession as a whole. It is also often confused with the caduceus, which is a staff entwined by two snakes with wings at the top. This is actually a symbol of commerce sacred to the god Hermes.

Coatlicue (Aztec)—This earth goddess is a creator and a destroyer, appearing in several different aspects, from a grandmother figure called Toci to a fertility figure known as Cihuacoatl (Snake Woman). She is portrayed in ancient art as being a large and fearsome woman with heavy breasts and a necklace made of human hands, hearts, and a skull. Her skirt is made from writhing snakes, and she is sometimes depicted as having a snake's head instead of a human one. The snake, with its ability to shed its skin, represents her connection to reincarnation, rebirth, and the Underworld.

Demeter (Greek)—This agricultural goddess is most concerned with the tides of the seasons, as they relate to the fertility of the land. Her chariot is drawn by a pair of winged serpents, and she is seen in ancient art holding sheaves of wheat in each hand with snakes twining around her wrists, indicating a connection to the cycles of birth, death, and rebirth. Snakes connect her to the Underworld, where her daughter Persephone spends half the year with Hades. Demeter came to be identified with the Roman goddess Ceres.

Hygeia (Greek)—As the daughter of Asklepios, god of medicine, it comes as no surprise that Hygeia joined the family business and became the goddess of good health. Some interpretations also credit her as a goddess of mental health in particular. A Greco-Roman statue dated from about the first century CE shows her holding a bowl in one hand and a snake in the other, which echoes her father's snake-entwined staff, the rod of Asclepius, which is the symbol for the medical profession. The word *hygiene* is derived from her name.

Qebhet (Egyptian)—Also known as Kebechet or Kebehwet, Qebhet is the daughter of Anubis and assists him in his duties of processing the deceased by offering them comfort and water as they await the judgement of Osiris. Originally honoured as a celestial snake deity with a body made of stars, she evolved into having a female body and the head of a snake or an entirely snake form.

Swallow

Vesna (Slavic)—A beautiful, buxom, and fertile goddess of rebirth, Vesna appears in the spring, after the death of Morana, the goddess of winter and death, with whom Vesna is forever entwined. She carries apples, grapes, and flowers along with her companion, a swallow, which represents her season.

Swan

Apollo (Greek)—Renowned for his incredible divine beauty and talent, Apollo is a god of the sun, music, poetry, healing, and divination. When he was born, his father, Zeus, gave him three gifts: a lyre, a golden mitre, and a chariot drawn by a bevy of swans. These birds also transport him to the mythical land of Hyperborea, a place that, depending on the version of the story, may be his original homeland or a place where he would go on retreat.

Brigid (Celtic)—Revered for her many faces, Brigid is a goddess of smithcraft, poetry, and midwifery, and it is in her role of the matron of childbirth that she is connected to the celestial stream of nourishing milk, the Milky Way, where the constellation of Cygnus, the swan, can be found. She is also associated with other white animals, including a white cow with red ears and an all-white bull.

Turtle

Enki (Sumerian)—This water deity is depicted in art as a man with flowing water running from his shoulders like a cloak. He is a trickster, and he rules art, mischief, virility, and creation. One of his great allies was a turtle that he made out of clay to help him teach a lesson in humility to Ninurta, a victorious hero and god of war and hunting. The turtle was brought to life by Enki and helped him trap Ninurta in a pit.

Wolf

Skadi (Norse)—Goddess of the winter and ice, Skadi, a giantess, is seen traveling the winter landscape on skis or snowshoes, hunting with spear or bow and arrow, in the company of wolves. When Skadi's husband, Njord, a god of wind and sea, comes to stay with her and complains about the howling wolves in the mountains, she instead welcomes the sound of her companions.

Leto (Greek)—One of the titans and the mother to Artemis and Apollo, Leto has been reported as either the first wife of Zeus or one of his lovers. In some stories, she is a she-wolf, while in others, she can shapeshift into wolf form; she gave birth to Apollo as a wolf pup. Her son is also strongly associated with wolves.

A World of Many Gods

Our world is filled with deities from a multitude of cultures, some that are still living and others that have become extinct. The list I have provided in this chapter is just a sample of the gods and goddesses that modern practitioners of witchcraft may be attracted to. In choosing the deities you work your witchcraft with, it is important to consider the context in which you are inviting them into your practice. Not all deities are from cultures or religions that recognize or tolerate witchcraft. If you do choose to work with a deity outside of your own culture, are you respecting and honouring them for who they are within their religion and historical context, or are you taking them and attempting to manipulate them for your own purpose?

As I mentioned at the beginning of this chapter, it is not essential to work with deities in order to practice witchcraft. Modern practitioners are so often encouraged to select deities from any cultural tradition they please and create new and inappropriate narratives and functions for them. Please consider looking to witchcraft folklore for deities and spirits that fit witchcraft practice or deities from your own cultural background first. If you choose to work with deities from living cultures other than your own, respect the existing customs and stories of those deities. Seek out the authentic stories from actual knowledge keepers and scholars and ensure that you are not misrepresenting or appropriating them to suit your own agenda.

PART TWO
Reimagining Magic Relationships with Animals

CHAPTER FIVE

Understanding the Natural Magic of Animals

At least once or twice every six months, a reoccurring question will pop up in one of the digital Pagan forums: "I keep seeing a (type of animal) and I want to know—what does this mean?"

The animal is usually something pretty ordinary sounding; more often than not it is a type of bird being asked about. As humans and as witches, we are often looking to nature for signs—something to give us wisdom or indicate that we are on the right path, but rarely do we take into consideration that the animal in question might just be there because it is normal for it to be there. It may not be about us and our need to be served by the situation after all.

Maybe it is because we have become out of touch with our natural world as our lives become more and more urbanized, and we are astounded by the presence and behaviour of wild creatures in our environment. Even in large cities, there are populations of wild animals that have come to live among us, even if we don't always notice them. Coming out under cover of the night around where I live, for example, there are raccoons, skunks, foxes, coyote, or deer right under my nose, camouflaged by their natural colouring, blending in with the cityscape, quite content to be safely ignored. When I am out walking with my dogs, it is very easy to walk past the deer that have infiltrated and set up housekeeping in my neighbourhood. They are like ghosts, their coats blending in perfectly with the trees. They are adept at standing stock-still, cloaking themselves in their environment so well that you have to really pay attention in order to see them. How many of us really pay attention? I mean *really* pay attention. When we do see wild animals in "human" environments, we are often caught off guard, surprised to see them in "our" space. Perhaps we need to adjust our perspective and remember that all spaces are as much for the wild things as they are for humans.

From a magical perspective, this coexistence with animals and the richness of sensory experience they possess can bring us real opportunity. Creating relationships with animals, whether wild, domestic, or of the spirit world, can offer us the opportunity to perceive the world of another being with a very different reality than our own. Like every other animal on earth, we humans live within our own bubble of reality. We see, hear, feel, smell, and taste in our unique human way. Every other animal species has their own way of perceiving the world, and each species has evolved to relate to it in a way that is unique to them. I will add that it is safe to assume that animals in the spirit world would likely maintain the same sense of perception that their counterparts in this material world experience. A dog spirit would still have that keen sense of smell that a physical dog has, for example. Being a creature of spirit in no way diminishes the sensory abilities the creature would have as a living, breathing animal.

The Worlds of Animals

We humans have a tendency to anthropomorphize animals, projecting human emotions or conditions onto them. That is to say that human beings limit their ability for relating to animals to human terms. We decide that the expression on our dog's face means that she is sad or that the cat who ignores us is a snob without considering what those behaviors actually mean in the language of the animal. We assume that because we can translate their behavior into a language that makes sense to us that we are correct, and we content ourselves with these assumptions. As a witch and a staunch believer in other realms, I see this as rather shortsighted. Through careful observation and practical study of animals, we can begin to learn how the animal is relating to its own world and draw on that creature's wisdom to expand our own vision of the world.

In 1909 German biologist Jakob Johann von Uexküll adopted the term *umwelt*, which translates from German as "environment," to describe an animal's perceptual world. He argued that despite all creatures sharing the same world, each species has a different perspective of its reality, or umwelt, based on how it had evolved to sense and experience it. Despite being in the same place, different animals, including humans, will experience the environment around them differently. For example, my dog Lola has the ability to smell odours that my human nose cannot detect. Her canine umwelt includes olfactory abilities that the human umwelt does not include. As a human, I cannot imagine what she is experiencing when she becomes very focused on a pile of something stinky and meticulously sniffs every little part of it. When I run her experience through my human filters, I am repulsed by her close examination of something I consider rotten and unpleasant. A dog's primary sense for understanding their environment is their sense of smell, and their brains are wired to detect information this way. Depending on breed, a dog's sense of smell can be 10,000 to 100,000 times more sensitive than our own. Their noses are equipped with as many as 100 million or more scent receptors, and when you compare this to our human noses with only up to six million scent receptors, you begin to understand why this sense is so important for our canine friends. I have come to learn and appreciate that for Lola to be happy and mentally stimulated, she needs to sniff. She needs to explore and enjoy her own umwelt just as much as I need to enjoy mine. Allowing her to have a good time out on a walk means slowing down to let her sniff and enjoy the experience. This allows for her to be a dog, using her senses as she naturally uses them. I have come to appreciate that it is as much her walk as my own, and maybe I need to slow down and take the time to smell something pleasant as well.

Uexküll wrote of his umwelt theory in his 1934 book titled *Streifzüge durch die Umwelten von Tieren und Menschen* (republished in English as *A Foray into the Worlds of Animals and Humans; with a Theory of Meaning*), which he introduced by explaining that access to the unseen world of other creatures was open to anyone who chose to accept the reality of the invisible worlds of other creatures. He wrote:

> **Everything a subject perceives belongs to its perception world [Merkwelt], and everything it produces, to its effect world [Wirkwelt]. These two worlds, of perception and production of effects, form one closed unit, the environment. The environments, which are as diverse as the animals themselves, offer every nature lover new lands of such richness and beauty that a stroll through them will surely be**

rewarding, even though they are revealed only to our mind's eye and not to our body's.[41]

What if the other realms we seek to work with as witches are more immanent than we originally thought? It has been a part of my training in witchcraft
to travel to other worlds. We speak of "outside the world, between the world,
and in all the worlds" and also of the Upper, Middle, and Lower Worlds. I agree
that these states exist, but I would argue that we are generally missing the boat
on our greatest opportunity to communicate with other worlds when we overlook the realities of the animals that we share the planet with. I am sure the
plant kingdom is doing the plant equivalent of rolling its eyes and wondering
when we will twig the realities they live in—but that would be another book.
By using our powers of imagination, visualization, and creativity, along with the
techniques of meditation and journeying, we can open a door between our own
umwelt and those of the creatures we are surrounded by.

The umwelten of other creatures does not limit the individual species to a
single confined version of reality. Indeed, other species are no doubt living as
fully and contentedly within their umwelten as we are within ours. I do not
possess the acute sense of smell that my dog Lola does, and she does not possess
the range of vision that I do. If we are playing together with a yellow tennis ball
at the park and another person and dog show up with an orange tennis ball, I
will be able to tell the two balls apart by looking at the colour, but to Lola those
particular colours appear undistinguishable from each other. Lola will rely on
her keen sense of smell to keep track of her tennis ball and can retrieve the correct one every time. If I was only allowed to find her ball by smelling it, I would
be at a complete loss. These are two different ways of perceiving the situation
that are both effective, and neither one of us is suffering any loss for not having
the other's ability.

Experiences like this with my dog Lola have taught me that by appreciat-
ing her perception of the world, I can have a wider appreciation of our shared
experiences. I can slow down and let her do her thing and appreciate her intelligence, trying to imagine the perspective she has on a given situation. I have

---

41. von Uexküll, *A Foray into the Worlds of Animals and Humans*, 42; brackets in the
    original.

widened my understanding of the environment around me by acknowledging that there are many perspectives that I cannot appreciate because I am a human that is not capable of perceiving them. Most creatures look at the world via the perspective of their own umwelten and leave it at that, humans included. What makes us different is that we humans also possess the capacity and the opportunity to become aware of and respect the umwelten of other species. This enables us to know and appreciate the visible and invisible world around us. As a witch I find this irresistible, and this makes my craft so much more immanent and accessible.

For a scientist, Uexküll was also quite the poetic writer as he described this phenomenon of widening our world by including the worlds of others like this:

> **We make a bubble around each of the animals living in the meadow. The bubble represents each animal's environment and contains all the features accessible to the subject. As soon as we enter into one such bubble, the previous surroundings of the subject are completely reconfigured. Many qualities of the colorful meadow vanish completely, others lose their coherence with one another, and new connections are created. A new world arises in each bubble.[42]**

As a witch this concept of umwelt and the revealing of the bubbles in which we all exist really appeals to me. Knowing that the creatures around me can see, hear, smell, or feel things that are beyond my own capacity fills me with a sense of wonder and magic, reminding me of why I have devoted my life to witchcraft in the first place. Science has so far only scratched the surface of what may be beyond our sensory capabilities, our umwelt. Just as the scientist can embrace the magic of poetry in his writing, so can we, the witches, include science in our magic—it is a fine line that divides the two. I am humbled by the idea that any one of the hundreds of thousands of so-called lower forms of life on this planet may be easily witnessing an unseen-by-humans perspective on reality that I do not even have the capacity to imagine. The behaviours that have been chalked up to "instinct" may well be a creature's unique intelligence sparking up and leading them into their own type of thought process—to migrate, to hunt, to

---

42. von Uexküll, *A Foray into the Worlds of Animals and Humans*, 43.

rear their young, or to seek shelter from a storm my local radio station weather reporter has yet to learn about from a satellite image. How often do you think about animals in these terms? I will warn you—once you do start to think about them in these terms, it is hard to stop. Adjusting your perspective like this is a road to a deeper way of magical thinking, of reprocessing the sensory information you receive on a daily basis in a greener, more natural, magical way. Watching a creature do something and then diving into how and why they do this from their point of view is like turning a key into a new world—one that exists right beside your own, if you dare to look.

Animal Perception

After reading this far, you may now understand how each different species of animal will have its own umwelt based on their own perception. Perception can be broken down into two key processes, the first being how sensory information is *detected* and the second being how this information is *organized*. Different animal species will have different detection and organization abilities, which determines how the information is perceived, creating their umwelt. The witchcraft we do with our animals in physical or spirit form will be stronger and more directed if we have an understanding of how the creatures we live and work with perceive the world and how that perception can complement our own. This can open up the toolbox of the relationship wider, exposing more possibilities for effective communication and deeper, more potent magic.

You may want to build a magical relationship with an animal that possesses abilities that complement your own—an animal with exceptional hearing may be helpful if your own hearing is impaired, or one that has excellent night vision may be of great assistance if you are like me and bumble around in low light. The following list of special abilities that animals possess is by no means exhaustive, but it will give you an idea of the potential available and the creatures that have them.

Echolocation

In order to survive in environments that are completely dark—or as nocturnal creatures—some animals have developed the ability to use echolocation to navigate in these challenging environments. The animals will use their voices to emit high-pitched sounds or clicking noises, often beyond the range of human hearing, that will bounce off objects and echo back so that the animals can use this information in order to map out where they are in relation to objects, surfaces, and even their prey.

Bats are the most famous creatures to have evolved this skill. They swoop easily through caves and caverns or outside at night, deftly avoiding obstacles thanks to muscles in their throats that enable them to create ultrasonic sounds and their ultrasensitive ears that can detect the echo bouncing back at them. They are able to determine the size, shape, and even the texture of obstacles in their environment using this technique. They are also able to hunt for their prey with this ability, catching insects in mid-flight.

Human beings who have lost their vision can sometimes develop a type of echolocation by listening to the way sound is moving around them in order to navigate their way in the world. This may not be exactly the same as the way animals do it, but it does get us closer to the idea of relying on a sense other than our eyes to move in the world.

I adore bats and like to evoke bat spirit when I am chanting and dancing during a group working with my coven. I will close my eyes as we move and chant, sometimes drumming as we raise energy together. I try to rely on my sense of hearing to tell me when I am too close to one of the other folks in the circle. This allows me a sort of freedom—my closed eyes help me get over my shyness about dancing in front of people—and I enjoy the sensation of allowing my ears to guide me. Strictly speaking, I am not echolocating, but I am navigating away from the sound of the other voices chanting in order to avoid a collision, which is about as close as my limited human witch-body can come.

Some animals that possess the ability to use echolocation are:

- Dormice
- Dolphins
- Whales
- Shrews
- Oilbirds
- Swiftlets
- Porpoises

Infrared

Infrared radiation is a part of the electromagnetic spectrum that human eyes cannot see. Some animals can see the infrared light that has longer wavelengths and lower energy than the visible spectrum. Warm-blooded animals like us can usually only experience infrared as the sensation of heat on our bodies, but some cold-blooded creatures are able to actually see infrared light. Insects that survive on drinking blood, such as bedbugs, ticks, and mosquitoes, rely on infrared to see the heat signature of the carbon dioxide gas that their prey exhales in order to locate them.

Do not get creeped out by the idea of working magic with crawly insects or slimy creatures. It may not work well to keep them as pets, but interacting with them in spirit form can give you a truly unique experience and maybe even a greater tolerance for creatures that usually make you uncomfortable in physical form. I have a phobia of wood ticks, but I will journey to meet ticks in spirit when I have a problem that I need to be small, tenacious, and "bloodthirsty" to solve. Ticks do not see shapes as we do; they rely instead on their ability to use infrared to pick up on the thermal signature of their targets. When my problem involves things being too abstract and confusing to see my way through, tapping tick spirit aids me to zone in on my answer by looking out for the trail it leaves behind, leading me to the source of the heat. Sometimes working with an animal familiar is about matching a metaphor to the work at hand and allowing yourself to follow it using the wisdom of the creature to guide you.

Some other creatures that use infrared are:

- Pit vipers
- Bullfrogs
- Salmon
- Goldfish
- Piranha
- Mantis shrimp

Infrasound

Deep below the range of human hearing is a world of sound that we can only imagine. In this soundscape there are the very low frequencies that are either barely discernible or not audible to us at all called infrasound. Unbeknownst to us, members of the animal kingdom are hearing or sensing information that gives them knowledge of the deepest workings of the earth and sky. Our limited hearing usually falls within a narrow band of frequencies between 20 Hz and 20 kHz. Infrasound falls below this range, so at best we may only be able to experience these sounds as a feeling of unease or pressure in the chest, trouble breathing, or digestive distress. When tests exposing human subjects to infrasonic frequencies have been run, the subjects reported feelings of anxiety, fear, and chills going down their spine. This is not unlike what happens at a big rock concert when you feel the bass hit you in the chest, affecting your breathing. I often wonder if my body is reacting to an infrasonic sound when I suddenly have an anxious or panicky feeling out of the blue, for no apparent reason. Is my witch-body detecting a signal that my human senses can't detect?

The source of these deep, far-reaching rumblings is often the earth itself—tectonic activity, storms, volcanoes, earthquakes, and crashing tides all cause the bones of the earth to shudder and throb. Some animals can actually hear these sounds, while others are much better than us at feeling them.

Have you ever noticed a dog behaving strangely just before a thunderstorm? My Oban used to get really uncomfortable and nervous, hiding behind furniture and refusing to go outside just before a storm. This was my cue, long before I could hear it and the rain and thunder arrived, that we were in for a noisy one.

A wide variety of animals can sense and sometimes even create infrasonic sound:

- Alligators
- Cod
- Elephants
- Giraffes
- Guinea fowl
- Hippopotamus
- Rhinoceros
- Squid
- Tigers
- Whales

Magnetoreception

Science defines magnetoreception as the ability some organisms have to detect the magnetic field of the earth. This is a possible explanation for how migratory birds know the routes they need to take, why sea turtles know how to return to the beach where they were born in order to lay their eggs, and how fish know the way to their spawning waters. The actual science on this is growing, and there is hope that with more understanding, we can learn how the earth's magnetic fields influence animals (including humans) and the environment. The study of this fascinates me and brings up the close connection between science and magic. If scientists are studying magnetoreception and witches and Pagans are discussing ley lines and earth energy—could we be talking about the same thing?

A very wide array of animals uses magnetoreception, and science has yet to figure out the mechanism by which each species detects and utilizes it. There has been research that indicates that humans may have a built-in system for detecting this energy and that our ancient ancestors would have used this ability for navigation.[43] If this proves correct, this presents an exciting opportunity for witches—an opportunity to reawaken this latent ability and use it to constructively do our magic. Many of us intuitively know that we can sense or feel energy, and by working with animals or animal energy that actively works with this same force, we can work on gaining a better understanding of it.

Here are some of the creatures of land, sea, and sky known to use magneto-reception as they travel and migrate:

- Bees
- Homing pigeons
- Deer
- Dogs
- Dolphins
- Newts
- Lobsters
- Migratory birds

43. Davis, "Pole Position."

- Rainbow trout
- Sharks

Night Vision

It is worth noting that many of the classic animals that are noted as witches' familiars have the ability to see in the dark better than humans. Perhaps this has something to do with the historic lore of witches moving about under the cover of night, going about their business as discreetly as possible under the light of the moon. Modern witches tend to prefer the later part of the day as well, as the evening hours offer the desired atmosphere and mystique, or maybe it's just more practical to get down to witchcraft when the workday is done and the kids are in bed.

The most common witchcraft animal, the cat, has the extraordinary ability to move about in very low light. The elliptical shape of their pupils enables them to open much wider than a human's round pupils, allowing them to maximize whatever light might be available. Cat eyes require only one-eighth of the light we need in order to function effectively thanks to reflective tissue they have behind their retinas called the *tapetum lucidum*. This same tissue is what causes their eyes to "glow" when caught in certain light.

Some popular animals that negotiate darkness adeptly include:

- Frogs
- Mice
- Opossums
- Owls
- Porcupines
- Raccoons
- Rats
- Red foxes
- Tarsiers

Scent and Smell

The ability to smell is the most basic and common way that animals communicate. They follow their noses—or whatever body part that they may use to detect scent—to find food or a mate, evade predators, or find their way home. They may produce a scent using their urine or glands in their bodies to mark their territory, scare off intruders, or indicate that they are in their fertile cycle. Human beings have a surprisingly good sense of smell, and some studies suggest that we are underestimating our natural abilities when we resign ourselves to not having as acute a sense of smell as most of the animal kingdom. Maybe we have just gotten out of the habit of needing this sense for survival, opting instead to be visual creatures, hooked on the abundance of visual stimulation we are inundated with in our technological age. When our senses of sight, hearing, touch, and taste are stimulated, that information goes into the thalamus, then it is relayed into the areas of the brain that will process it. But when we smell something, the scent goes straight into our olfactory bulb, immediately triggering the parts of our brains that hold memories and emotions. It is more direct and can have an intense effect. Knowing this is a powerful tool for a witch and working with your own sense of smell can be a powerful aid to draw you into a magical state of mind. Does the smell of lavender remind you of your grandmother? Now by the same process, does the scent of a certain incense immediately pull you into a ritual frame of mind? Working with an animal familiar or companion animal with a keen sense of smell can widen that range with you. You will not be able to detect what the animal can, but you can watch them for signs that they are onto something beyond your range.

You can also work with the energy of an animal to enhance your ability to "sniff out" a problem, or you may call upon the animal's ability to smell in order to divine the location of a missing person or object. For example, if I was trying to determine where I had lost something and I knew it could be anywhere in a large area, I may call an elephant spirit. Make your selection based on how suitable the animal is for the terrain and conditions you are dealing with.

Some animals you can connect with that have a keen sense of smell are:

- Bears
- Cows
- Dogs

- Elephants
- Kiwis
- Moles
- Sharks
- Silkworm moths
- Snakes
- Turkey vultures

Tactile Perception

Are you a hugger? What is the value of a handshake, a pat on the back, or a soft caress on the cheek? For us humans, our sense of touch and how we use it varies widely. For the animal kingdom, touch is often a basic survival tactic. Tactile communication may be used for bonding, greeting, establishing dominance, or hunting, and it is fascinating to see what styles of communication cross the boundaries between different species and which ones have different meanings. Nuzzling, pawing, licking, wrestling, biting, and body-to-body contact are all techniques animals use to communicate using touch.

My old cat, Roddy, adored my dog Oban. The two of them would cuddle and sleep together. Roddy would contentedly groom Oban, meticulously licking Oban's ears clean, purring as he worked away. In return, Oban would nuzzle Roddy, nibbling and biting him along his belly as if he was a cob of corn. This was their daily routine, and they both appeared to not only enjoy it but actively seek it out. Both cats and dogs are social animals that use tactile communication as a form of social bonding. They will use grooming and playful biting as a way to develop the bonds needed to ensure survival, and both cats and dogs will extend this to other species that they need to bond with in order to survive.

Animals can also have body parts that give them tactile sensations that we aren't capable of. A cat's whiskers, for example, transmit tactile sensations down to the nerves in the hair follicle. These messages can be a subtle change in air flow or a rub against a hard object. Without this information, the cat would not be as adept at navigating in the dark.

By understanding the tactile language of the animals we want to work with, we can incorporate techniques for physical contact that is pleasurable and nonthreatening to our pets and animal companions, and we can incorporate movements that will not be seen as threatening or exerting dominance to our animals of body as well as those of spirit.

Animals that use tactile perception to relate to other animals include:

- Bears
- Felines, domestic and wild
- Canines, domestic and wild
- Deer
- Dolphins
- Gulls
- Horses
- Otters
- Monkeys
- Rabbits

Ultraviolet

Ultraviolet radiation is also a part of the electromagnetic spectrum that has shorter wavelengths and higher energy than the visible spectrum that most humans can see. The sun is our natural source of ultraviolet (UV) energy, which has the benefit of producing vitamin D, but overexposure to UV can cause health problems such as cancer or eye problems. We have evolved to have lenses in our eyes that filter out UV light, so it's usually only people who have lost their lenses to cataracts or accidents, for example, who may be able to detect UV, seeing it as a whiteish violet light, and get a sense of what the world might look like to the animals that have evolved to see it easily.

Insects that feed on flowers can see the UV light that is reflected by the flowers, and in some cases, they have UV markings on their bodies that help them attract suitable mates. Many species of birds also use UV markings to find mates. In some species of birds, both males and females look alike until our human eyes look at them using a spectrophotometer, a tool that allows us to see UV light. With this perspective it is easy to tell the birds apart as they have markings that clearly distinguish the males form the females—if only you have the eyes to see them.

Have you ever watched a cat stare into a corner or at a blank wall so intently that you could believe they were looking at some kind of ghost or supernatural being? It may just be that they are watching patterns of UV light play across the surface. Cats, and dogs, too, are among the creatures that can see UV light. This really helps them hunt and navigate in low light as the UV makes a wider spectrum of light available to them to operate by. For a witch to work with animals such as these in physical or spirit form, there is the opportunity to widen the spectrum of vision for your magical work. With physical animals you can observe how they are perceiving your shared environment, and with animal familiars, you can journey to their world and visualize their perspective for yourself.

Some additional animals that can see ultraviolet light are:

- Barn swallows
- Bees
- Butterflies
- Hedgehogs
- Iguanas
- Rats
- Reindeer
- Scorpions
- Spiders
- Turtles

WORKING
Journey to Discover the Umwelt of Another Animal

One of the tools in a witch's toolbox is the power to use a type of meditation called journeying to travel to realms that our physical bodies are unable to access. This process will require you to have a specific, focused intention and then to allow yourself to enter into a trance state. This trance state can feel light, like a daydream, or it can get to be as intense as a full-on out-of-body experience. If you are new to this technique, take things slowly until you have a sense of how this feels for you. You may need to try this working a few times before you feel satisfied that it works for you, so do not be discouraged if that is the case; this is normal.

The purpose of this working is to journey to the umwelt of an animal and gain some insight into how another creature, be they spirit or physical, sees the world. You will need to do some research and make some notes in order to prepare.

Select an Animal

Start by spending some time choosing an animal to focus on. I would challenge you to select one that is not your usual go-to animal. If you, like me, are a dog person, rule that one out right away. Is there a wild animal in your environment that you see regularly but don't know much about? Is there an animal that appears in your dreams on a regular basis? This may be a good place to start. Picking up on the umwelt of an animal that already shares your environment may prove to be a good learning experience for you. If you get stuck or just can't pick one, try using your favourite form of divination to help you choose.

Once you have settled on the animal you will be working with for this exercise, do a bit of research to find out some information about their world. Ask the following questions and make some notes about the answers:

- What is their habitat?
- What do they eat?
- What is their vision like?
- How acute is their hearing?
- Are they nocturnal (active during the night) or diurnal (active during the day)?
- Are they migratory? Do they hibernate?
- How do they move?
- What sounds do they make?

Spend some time observing your chosen animal. This should preferably be done with the animal in their natural habitat, but if that is not possible, find some videos or pictures online or study pictures of it in books. Read up on their behaviour, eating habits, mating habits, and life cycle. Once you feel you have a sense of the facts about this animal, move on to the next step: preparing yourself for the journey.

Prepare for the Journey

To begin your journey and enter a trance state, you will need to have a quiet place where you can be undisturbed. Allow yourself at least an hour to complete this working. It helps to dim the lights, and make sure that the ringer is turned off on your phone. Set up a comfortable place where you can sit or lie down comfortably. Wear something that does not pinch or restrict you and that will keep you comfortably warm or cool depending on your needs. I tend to get quite cool when I journey and find that having a blanket to wrap around me helps me relax.

If you are able to record yourself reading the following journey, you can play it back to guide yourself through it. I find that the voice memo feature on my phone is handy for this sort of thing. When recording, pause between sentences and do not rush through the words. Allow for time for the words to sink in as you listen to them during your journey.

If recording doesn't work for you, try writing it out in point form and propping it up where you can easily read it to prompt yourself. I find that I can do this fairly effectively if I allow my eyes to close slightly and softly focus on my notes in low light. If you are good at memorizing things, you can try that; I find I think too much when I work from memory, so some kind of outside prop or recording to stay on track really helps. Recruiting a fellow witch to talk you through the journey also works really well, and then you can return the favour and be a guide for them.

The Journey

Settle yourself into a comfortable position, either sitting or lying down. Breathe in for a count of four, hold for a count of four, exhale for a count of four, then hold for a count of four. Repeat until you feel relaxed and at peace. Begin your journey by allowing yourself to sink down, down into the warmth and safety of the green earth. Take a moment to appreciate the comfortable embrace of the great green earth. You arrive in a green and beautiful landscape, a natural place where your chosen creature can be found. As you look around, you become aware that your chosen creature has ventured close to you. Observe the creature from every angle. Hold the image in your mind until it becomes crystal clear. When the creature moves, allow your astral body to move with it, joining in with the creature's movement and flow. When the movement feels natural to you, ask the creature if you may experience their world. Tell them you will not stay long and that you will respect their autonomy. Allow your astral body to gently merge with the creature. Allow the creature's movements to be your movements, their breath to be your breath. How does this feel? Allow your eyes to see as they do. What can you see? Allow your ears to hear as they do. What can you hear? Allow your appetite to be as theirs is. What do you hunger for? Allow your instinct to be as theirs is. What do you need to do? Give yourself a few minutes to experience this perspective of the world. Internalize the sights, sounds, and sensations that your animal is sharing with you. Explore their umwelt, allowing the sensory experiences to imprint on you. When it is time to depart, thank the creature for the experience of their perspective. Gently unmerge your astral body from the astral body of the creature. Your breath is your own breath. Your movements are your own movements. You see, hear, hunger, and need to do your regular things now. The creature moves free, unaffected by the journey together. You move free, wiser and stronger from the journey together. You stand in the green and beautiful place, and then move back to our world, ready to make notes about what you have experienced. Take three deep breaths and return to your normal state of being. Write down what you have experienced and learned about the sensory world of your chosen creature.

On Their Terms

Working with animals in physical or spirit form needs to be a collaborative, constructive relationship, and it is kinder and more productive to work on speaking the same language and respecting their intelligence. Knowing that animals have these abilities and that they can see, hear, smell, taste, and touch these things that we can't, wakes up a richer, wider world around us. This landscape that we share is humming with these things—infrared light, a new depth and richness of scents, swirling trails of vibration and current, fields of magnetism, and tactile sensation—that are all beyond what we can experience, or even catalogue, as humans. When we sense the vitality and richness of the planet, when we stand in nature, awestruck by the vibrance and life force around us, our own extrasensory perception is hovering just out of reach of a kaleidoscope of what is also out there. The overlapping layers of the other realities, the umwelten, of other creatures are all around us, each one being equally mysterious and precious as the next, and all of these realities need to be respected and preserved. For all the benefit, joy, and mystery that this can bring, it is also a precious resource that can be trampled and lost. We cannot begin to understand the multitudinous layers of connection between the visible and invisible realms of our world. As a human community, we are doing a lousy job of protecting and preserving the natural world that we can see, let alone valuing the aspects of it that are invisible to us. When we lose a species to extinction, we also lose the umwelt of that species, and the richness of the natural tapestry that we are cloaked in becomes a bit paler. It is a loss of diversity, of life, and of the unseen world of that species and its mysteries. This presents another opportunity to witches and magical practitioners, an opportunity to do good work to preserve and protect the whole tapestry of life, seen and unseen.

CHAPTER SIX
Receiving Animal Wisdom

Throughout history, human beings have made decisions based on messages received from animals. The lives of our hunter-gatherer ancestors depended on their ability to find and hunt their prey, so being able to read the evidence left by animals, such as tracks, feces, or other remnants of their movements, was a basic survival skill. Over time, cultures developed different methods for using live animals, or parts of dead ones, to perform acts of divination to determine the past, present, and future.

Theriomancy, sometimes also referred to as zoomancy, is the art of divining messages from the behaviour or appearance of living animals. Unfortunately not all types of animal divination involved the animal living to talk about it. Haruspicy, a form of divination that involves reading the entrails of a sacrificial animal, was developed and practiced by the ancient Etruscans, who lived in what is now Italy. They believed that the will of the gods could be relayed by the haruspex, a specifically trained person who would read the patterns in the internal organs of mainly sheep and chickens, although just about any type of physical animal could be used.[44]

My late grandmother would often make comments about the pattern of birds in flight, making comments like "three birds mean friendship, two birds mean love" when she would see them flying into her backyard. This would be an example of augury, or the interpretation of the patterns of birds. Augury is just one form of animal divination that is observational and relatively easy to practice.

---

44. de Grummond, "Haruspicy and Augury."

For reference, here is a list of some additional examples of animal divination:

- **Ailuromancy (also known as felidomancy):** Foretelling the future by observing the movements of cats
- **Alectryomancy:** Divination by observing how a rooster pecks at grain or lettered tiles scattered on the ground
- **Augury:** Divination by observing the patterns of birds; ancient Romans had a very developed system for this that employed an augur, an official interpreter of the signs, to relay messages from the gods.
- **Batraquomancy:** Divination by frogs, toads, and sometimes newts, primarily to predict weather
- **Canomancy:** Divination by dog movements and behaviour
- **Hippomancy:** Divination that interprets the behaviour of a living horse or the bones of a dead one; it can also involve reading patterns in the tracks they make or the sound of their neighing.
- **Ichthyomancy:** Divination by observing the patterns of fish swimming, either in the wild or in a consecrated bowl or pond
- **Myomancy:** Divination by the movements, vocalizations, or damage caused by mice and rats
- **Myrmomancy:** Divination to determine past, present, or future events by studying the behaviour and appearance of ants or termites
- **Nggàm:** Originating in Cameroon, this divinatory technique involves spiders or crabs and how their movements affect a set of "cards" made out of leaves and small sticks.
- **Ololygmancy:** Divination by interpreting the pattern of the barking and howling of dogs
- **Ophiomancy:** Divination by the colour and movement of snakes
- **Plastromancy:** Originating in ancient China, this form of divination involved heating the under shell, or plastron, of a turtle until it cracked and then reading the pattern of the cracks for messages.

- **Skatharomancy:** Divination that involves reading the patterns made in the tracks that beetles leave in dirt or dust
- **Spatilomancy:** Divination by reading patterns in animal excrement

These practices involve using animals more than collaborating with them. The animal is passive in the process and is being "read" as they just go about their business, or they are ritually killed to get a message from their bodies. Observation does no harm to the animal and can be a fun and interesting way to gain some insight and learn more about animal behaviour. Ritual sacrifice is absolutely not called for or necessary in order to gain insight. These practices should be avoided and remain a part of human history, not the present.

Animal Telepathy

Anyone who has lived with a truly beloved pet or companion animal may understand what I mean by animal telepathy. The animals in our lives do seem to have the ability to understand our feelings and moods or even our state of health. Domestic pets, such as cats and dogs, tend to stick close by our sides when we are sick or upset. Happiness and expressions of joy seem contagious to any animals in the house, and they usually want to be in the middle of an exciting family moment. Without being told, without using words or language, our pets and animal companions have the ability to pick up on the energy we are projecting and mirror it back to us.

In 2008 I attended a Pagan conference and met a woman who was offering her services as an animal communicator to conference delegates for a special rate. In a moment of impulsiveness, I hired her services. The deal was that we would have a phone meeting in a couple weeks and following that she would undertake a type of journey to meet Oban on the astral plane and communicate with him. I was skeptical that this would result in much, but she seemed 100-percent committed to the process and was extremely sweet and passionate about her calling as a pet psychic.

A couple weeks later, we met on the phone and had a discussion about the process. She asked me a few basic questions about Oban—his age, size, and breed. I did disclose that he was epileptic, on two kinds of meds for this and that I was worried about how the meds made him feel. Could she tell me if he liked his food? Is he in any pain?

The animal communicator then said she was reaching out to Oban right now, connecting with him as she and I spoke on the phone. Her voice got rather dreamy, which made me roll my eyes... until I looked at Oban. He was in the middle of the hallway, sitting quite upright and staring into space as if listening to someone that was standing in front of him. It made my hair stand on end to see him so transfixed. The animal communicator translated some of Oban's "words" to me, then announced that this communication was over for now—she had made a date to reach out to Oban again in a couple of days. As soon as she said this, Oban snapped out of his trance and wandered over to the sofa and jumped up next to me. OK—maybe something IS going on here.

Ten days later, the communicator and I spoke again on the phone and went over her conversations with Oban. She had agreed to have one session but ended up having three because he was such a "gentleman" and they had enjoyed each other's company. There were a number of things that did not resonate with me, but then there were also a number of details that she could not possibly have known without someone telling her. For example, Oban liked his food but did not like the "smoke-flavoured thing" I put in it. He said he would eat it anyway because I told him it was good for him. I was surprised by this as I thought I was being clever, hiding his smoky bacon-flavoured vitamin in his evening meal. Oban also expressed that he was concerned by the number of times he saw me using Rescue Remedy, something I discreetly would use at work.

The animal communicator was most impressed by the poem that Oban wrote for me. She had only ever experienced poetry from a horse before, so dog poetry was a very exciting development for her.

To my
Doe ray me
To my amie
De cour
To my
Sous aux yeux
De feu
To my doe ray me

**To my
Dodie**

My friends and I had often joked that Oban had the soul of a poet, and as you can read in his poem, he was no Pablo Neruda, but it was very heartfelt and sweet nonetheless.

Omens

The sudden and unexpected appearance of an animal can sometimes feel like a message. It could be a wild animal that pops up when you least expect it or a beloved pet doing something out of character. As tempting as it may be to believe that this is some kind of omen, it is important to remember that what you are seeing might just be an animal being itself, going about its business, and not trying to communicate with you at all. Bearing this in mind, if your gut and witch's instinct are telling you that this appearance is meaningful, unusual, and important, it probably is.

An omen, strictly speaking, is an event that indicates something about the future. These occurrences are often interpreted to be messages or prophecies from the spirit world and may be referred to as "good" or "bad" omens depending on the circumstances. To this I will argue that anything that gives you a glimpse into your future can only be positive because you still have the free will to work on changing undesired outcomes. Always remember that as witches, we have the self-determination to use our skills to achieve our desired outcomes.

To determine whether an animal's appearance is, in fact, an omen, consider these factors:

- Is it normal for this animal to be here? If the location is nowhere near its native habitat, that is notable.
- Is the animal displaying its typical behaviour? The animal may be sick, frightened, or injured, so try to rule that out before reading anything mystical into the situation.
- Does the animal have its usual appearance? The sudden appearance of a white raven would be more of an omen than the appearance of a regular black one, for example.

- Is the animal alive or dead? Happening upon the corpse of a dead creature can indicate a message from the Underworld.

- How did the animal react to you? Being comfortable with your presence would be notable, as wild animals are more likely to shy away from humans.

- Was the animal an aquatic, terrestrial, or flying creature? The element the animal was in may have a bearing on the nature of the omen or message it was bringing you.

- What were you doing when the animal appeared? If you were lost in thought, daydreaming, or meditating, this may make the potency of an unexpected encounter affect you on a deeper level.

- What was your initial reaction to seeing this animal? Try to remember what your spontaneous reaction and thoughts were upon encountering the creature.

Be as honest as you possibly can when you work through these questions, and try to do so without overthinking or projecting your desired outcome onto the situation. When you feel like the information "clicks" and you have a moment of feeling that you have reached truth, stop there. As spontaneous as the appearance of your message-bringer was, your interpretation should rest just as quickly, without nit-picking or second guessing your instinct and intuition.

Divination with Physical Animals

We can receive messages from any living animal, whether they are a pet, an animal companion, or a wild animal. As we can see in the list of types of animal divination used for millennia by humans from cultures around the world, it is completely natural for us to turn to the animal kingdom for guidance in times of need.

Such messages need not involve an intermediary, as in my story about Oban, but they will usually involve paying attention and being receptive to information that may come from unusual sources. A common theme for interpreting these messages is the observation of patterns and determining what they represent. As in the example of augury that my grandmother used to cite, a pair of birds meant love. This is a reasonable conclusion as it takes two birds to make a mating pair, and it is no great leap to imagine that seeing two together means they are indeed such a pair. Three birds are a small group and may imply a more casual, friendly relationship. Using this sort of logic, you can create your own system of divination to read the wildlife outside your door. All you need are some critters and a symbolic language to draw from.

For those of us who practice witchcraft, we are pretty well equipped with a symbolic language that we can use to interpret the signs and signals we get from animals. Witchcraft has a distinct language of its own, with words that you may only ever read in a book or hear spoken within witchcraft groups. This is an opportunity to look to your practice and tradition and give some thought to the symbols, correspondences, and associations that you use and apply them to the patterns and behaviours of the animals that you observe.

Here is a sample list of the associations I use based my own witchcraft practice:

Moving deosil	Animals moving clockwise indicating a raising of energy, excitement, or anticipation; positive movement
Moving widdershins	Animals moving counterclockwise indicating a depletion of energy or resources; things not progressing as desired
One animal	Solitary—self-sufficiency, ability to do whatever needs to be done alone
Two animals	Working partners—a successful partnership of like minds, able to amplify and enhance each other's magic or potential
Three animals	Minimum number for a coven—community, friendship, family
Positioned in the east	Realm of thought and intellect—what ideas, concepts, language, or discussion is required? Dawn, new beginnings

Positioned in the south	Realm of action—what needs to be done? Midday, fulfillment
Positioned in the west	Realm of emotions—what is being felt, dreamed of, or intuitively learned? Sunset, endings
Positioned in the north	Realm of the physical world—what is the foundation? What basic needs must be met? Night, darkness, repose
Positioned in the centre	Realm of deities—what is the message the gods want you to hear?

WORKING
Divination with Local Wildlife

This working is intended as a way to gain insight on a situation or question you may have by observing the wildlife in your area. The key is to trust your intuition, not overthink it, and use correspondences that you are already familiar with. Numbers, colours, time of day, and directions are a good start and are universal enough to help you get some answers to your queries. You can refer to the table of associations I have already provided to get you started.

To begin, identify wildlife that is local to you. Depending on where you live, this could be birds, rodents, insects, lizards, or any number of small mammals. Observe them over a period of a few days so that you get a sense of how they behave. This may be as easy as observing out of your window, or you may have to head outside and explore a bit to find what you are looking for.

Once you have a handle on how the animals behave and where you can reliably find them, focus on a question or situation that you need some insight to understand. With this set firmly in your mind, turn your attention to what the animals you have been observing are doing and make some notes:

- How many animals can you see?
- Do they appear calm, aggressive, playful, asleep, etc.?
- Are they interacting with other animals?
- Are they young or mature animals?
- If they are moving, what direction are they moving? For example, are they moving deosil or widdershins?
- Are they exhibiting a particular behaviour—grooming, eating, nesting, mating, etc.?
- Does the animal look directly at you?
- Are they doing anything unexpected based on your previous observations?
- Does the animal appear healthy, content, frightened, etc.?

Make note of anything about the behaviour that you observe that catches your eye. Once you have your list of observations, you can use it to divine an answer to your query.

Here is an example of what I mean: I have a large number of rabbits in my neighbourhood and a colony lives under the juniper bush in my front yard, so it is hardly unusual for me to see a number of rabbits on a daily basis. I have observed them long enough that I have a good general sense of what urban rabbits do and how they behave. With my query clearly formed in my mind, I keep my eye out for the rabbits and make note on what I observe. Then, I use the associations from my witchcraft practice to help me interpret the rabbit behaviour. For example:

Three rabbits grazing on grass on the west side of the yard = at the end of the day, a feeling of contentment for the group, ending with the fuel needed for a good outcome.

In this example, we have the number three, the minimum number you need to form a coven. The rabbits are in the west, the direction associated with the evening and the emotional realm. The rabbits eating together represents the feast, a time of hospitality and the company of good friends and fellow witches.

Had the rabbits appeared in the east, the direction associated with air, the realm of thought and intellect, I might interpret that as meaning that the group should brainstorm together and think about a better course of action. In the south, realm of fire, there would need to be a group action to move on, quick like a bunny, and in the north, realm of earth, the group should stand their ground and enjoy the abundance of the present moment.

This exercise is very helpful for not only getting some insight to the questions or situations you need help with, but it can also help you make a stronger connection to the natural world.

Messages Received

For all the documented types of divination or communication methods involving animals there may be, there is no one correct way. It comes down to personal style, comfort level, and the relationship you want to build with the animals in your environment. The key is to create an understanding of the animals you are observing, be objective about natural versus unusual behaviour, and pay attention to patterns. Read the animals as they appear naturally; do not go out looking for them. The context in which they reveal themselves can be part of the message.

The animal message may show up in unexpected ways as well. A feather laying on your path, an image on a greeting card that arrives unexpectedly in the mail, or a seashell found nowhere near a body of water—these could be read as messages from the animal kingdom as well.

These techniques and practices may offer you a new way to tap into the natural magic of animals and appreciate, on a very intimate level, how interconnected our lives are with other creatures and the pulse of nature itself.

CHAPTER SEVEN
Seeking Familiars & Companions

The relationships we have with animals, be they in spirit or physical form, all need to start with a meeting. This is straightforward and much easier to do with physical animals as there are so many options and places to go to adopt or purchase them. Sometimes they even choose us by following us home or turning up unannounced on our doorsteps and just somehow end up staying forever. Meeting an animal familiar can be trickier. For this you will need to try some deliberate techniques, watch for subtle clues, and objectively follow your intuition. No matter what form they come in, you will need to be prepared to give your attention, support, and love to any animals that you invite to share your magical and mundane life with.

Seeking a Familiar

The animals in the spirit world that we want to connect and build familiar relationships with can be elusive and hard to find. This can be frustrating at times, but it is intensely rewarding when you are able to have an authentic, tangible meeting with the energy and influence of an animal familiar. It is so important to be pragmatic and realistic in your seeking, as working with spirits of any kind can be a pursuit that can be subject to delusion. Make sure you take into account that the reality of a familiar does not often look like the fantastical impressions we can get from reading books or surfing the internet. I think of this the same way that I think about the difference between witches in real life and witches in fairy tales or movies—the reality is much more subtle and ordinary looking than the stories. The reality of working with an animal familiar will likely be more subtle and nuanced than what you might expect as well. Instead of having a fully materialized, talking, spectral animal doing your bidding and dispensing arcane wisdom, you will need your intuition, observational skills, and powers of visualization to interact with your familiar. It will also be helpful to develop the ability to journey, remember your dreams, and practice a form divination to enhance your communication with them.

Recognizing the Experience

The quest to meet your own familiar animal may have already happened and you just haven't realized it yet. This is what happened to me—I was looking too hard and had so many preconceived notions that I didn't immediately recognize what had happened. I had to take a step back, reflect, and have a couple of important conversations to put some context around my experience. Despite having a pretty open mind, my own skeptical nature sabotages my magical experiences sometimes.

After many lukewarm attempts at using the technique of journeying, various forms of meditation, and even divination to locate my own animal familiar, nothing had happened. I took some shamanic practitioner training workshops and seemed to be the only person in the group that wasn't getting dramatic visions of ravens, wolves, or owls. I am definitely not the type to be comfortable with the technique of "dancing your animal guide," but I tried it anyway, afraid I might dance up a funky chicken. I resigned myself to not having an animal familiar. I left the door open to the possibility that it could happen and left it at that.

A few years went by, and I found myself on a work trip to the remote northern community of Churchill, Manitoba. This small town of roughly 800 people is located on the coast of Hudson Bay, at the mouth of the Churchill River, and it is known as the Polar Bear Capital of the World. I was up in Churchill working on a documentary about polar bears. Any concerns I may have had about not seeing any bears were quickly dashed as the bears were plentiful and sightings frequent.

Part of my job was driving a pickup truck and following the camera vehicle, standing by on my walkie-talkie in case the crew needed anything, and watching out for bears, of course. It was late October, when the bears start to stage themselves along Hudson Bay, just outside of town, to wait for the ice to come in so they can head out on the frozen water to hunt seal, and to say I was blown away by seeing polar bears in the wild is an understatement. After my first day following them around, I was most impressed by how they would sit facing the bay, waiting. I spent many hours watching how they would sit so still, so meditatively, watching for some unknown-to-me sign that the ice was coming in.

After a couple of nights, I started to dream about polar bears. They were not the subject of the dreams, but they were in the periphery, watching me have my dreamtime experience. Then on the third night, polar bears were stalking me. Gliding out of nowhere, from behind boulders and snowbanks, bears snorting and huffing, paws whumping on the snow. One large bear appeared directly in front of me, and as it walked directly at me, I opened my arms to accept whatever may happen. The dream-bear was huge and walked right through my body, and I was paralyzed. Then, suddenly there was a terrific banging sound directly outside my window, and I woke up and jumped to see what was happening. It was about 3 a.m. and the Manitoba conservation officers, who are in charge of chasing off nosy polar bears who come into town, were firing bear bangers into the sky to scare off a lumbering polar bear who had been right outside my window! As I had been dreaming, an actual bear was on the other side of the wall, nosing around.

I related my dreams to my host. She said that bears come to us in the Dreamworld to remind us to respect their territory and boundaries. They speak to us in these liminal spaces to check us out and bring us messages from their world.

My dreams continued every night I was in Churchill. I was also routinely woken up by the sound of more bear bangers chasing them out of town.

Since then, I still get regular visits from one particular polar bear, and I have come to recognize him (and I say "him" because he is quite large; females are usually considerably smaller) as my animal familiar. He visits me in my dreams, usually when I am in need of advice or support with a magical working and especially if I am feeling vulnerable. I also get a strong sense of him when I am walking outside, usually in a natural place and most often in winter. During my meditative walks, I can audibly hear his paws hitting the ground and the sound of him sniffing the air. If I try to look directly at him, the connection breaks. I quickly learned that this is a relationship on his terms. His comfort zone is in the periphery.

The first few times the bear appeared, it was unnerving, but now I am reassured by these encounters, and I miss him if we go too long between visits. I used to be worried he wouldn't come back, but now I trust he will. I wrote off my initial contact with my animal familiar as "just a dream" and as an "extraordinary coincidence," even though my gut was telling me something else.

Ways to Meet an Animal Familiar

I'm not going to lie—all through my quest to meet an animal familiar, I was holding on to the cherished outcome that my animal familiar would be a great big stag with a huge rack of antlers and a retro 1980s "Robin of Sherwood" vibe about him. But it was just not happening. Looking back at it now, I believe that I was trying too hard, not trusting my instincts and not using the tools that my witchcraft practice provides me with. My seeking for an animal familiar was overshadowed by my own preconceived notions and other people's expectations.

In historic accounts, witches met their animal familiars in much more dramatic ways than what I experienced. Folklore and historic records tell us that witches could be given a familiar by the Devil in exchange for loyalty or their soul, or they may receive one from an elder witch as an inheritance upon their death. Witches may have been approached by the familiar and offered assistance with a problem in exchange for a meal of the witch's blood and a nice place to live.

These historic stories may be relatable for some modern witches, but for most, meeting a familiar is a little less dramatic. Modern witches can use a variety of techniques to initiate contact with an animal familiar and use more conventional means to meet these guides than their historical counterparts did. If these techniques don't work out as hoped, you may find yourself, as I did, giving up and focusing on other things and letting the familiar choose the time and place to introduce themselves. As my own experience has taught me, you need to pay attention, read the signs, and not block a real opportunity because it doesn't meet your expectations. Discussing what your experiences are, either with other practitioners or folk who are sympathetic to the natural world, also really helps. Being grounded and pragmatic about your expectations and experiences while on this quest is important. Here are some practices you can use to help you on your search:

Keep a Journal

Don't you roll your eyes. Keeping a journal really works, and it doesn't need to be heavy, overly detailed, or long-winded. Making daily notes about patterns and occurrences around you can be extremely helpful with all sorts of magic. I keep a spiral-bound notebook at my desk. I write my to-do lists in it and note anything else significant going on in my life. I never write more than a line or two about anything, but I do make a point of documenting patterns that come up, weather, moon phases, and anything else that triggers a gut reaction. Dreams, messages that come through while drawing tarot cards, something in my horoscope that strikes a nerve, astrological occurrences, and even particular food cravings go into the book. Along with including this sort of information, make notes about the animals you see throughout your day, migratory species you may have observed, or evidence that animals had been in a place you visited. Did you see any animal tracks? Geese flying north or south overhead? Squirrels gathering nuts, or birds building a nest? Just a few words about things like this is enough to establish a pattern. Being able to go back and read over your own notes is a great way to pick up clues about and signs of your animal familiar.

Analyze Your Witchcraft Practice

Your animal familiar may be trying to get your attention in subtle ways, reaching out to you through your magical practice. Take a look around your home, focusing on the areas in it dedicated to witchcraft—your altars, bookshelves, art, jewelry, and ornaments, for example.

- Do you honour a deity that has a specific animal associated with them?
- Do you use magical tools made out of a particular type of animal?
- Is there a food product made from animals that you consume as part of your witchcraft practice?
- Do you wear clothing or jewelry that depicts specific animal imagery?
- Have you incorporated statuary or art of a particular animal into your ritual space?
- Do friends and family who know you well gift you items that depict a certain animal?

All of these things could indicate that you are already working with an animal familiar in an unconscious and informal way. The animal familiar may be using these repeated patterns to let you know that they are there and willing to work with you.

In the story at the beginning of this chapter, I described meeting my polar bear familiar. In his honour, I have acquired some polar bear art that I display in my home, but in my temple room, you can't turn your head without seeing representations of deer. Despite my desired stag familiar never appearing to me in any dramatic or tangible ways, these animals are such a huge part of my witchcraft practice. My strong affinity for these animals can be found on my altar, decorating the walls, in the jewelry I wear, and depicted on an embarrassing abundance of tools and ornaments. There is a strong connection to the spirit of deer as a familiar animal, despite me not having the same type of vivid and profound experiences I have had with the polar bear. But then, deer are quieter, gentler creatures then polar bears—in spirit as well as in the physical world.

Read and Research

For every location on the planet, there is printed information available about the flora and fauna of that region. Reading up on the wildlife native to your area is a great way to establish an affinity with a type of animal that could become your familiar, and it also provides you with a good base of knowledge of your bioregion, which is essential for any witch to be fluent in. Some of the books I reference most for my witchcraft aren't books about witchcraft at all. Instead, they are field guides, natural history books, and books of nature photography, local history, and folklore. These resources satisfy my curiosity and also educate me in the natural cycles of the land I live on, giving me a better understanding of how the local wildlife lives and what it needs in order to thrive. All of these books will present you with a background for creating sympathy with animals in your landscape. Localizing your witchcraft this way makes it more immanent, more immediate, and very practical, allowing you to work with the reality of your surroundings and the world you actually live in. There was a time when witch books gave knowledge and information largely based on climate and landscape that was alien to most of us reading them. This is not the case anymore, and we can absolutely tap a wider pool of resources to empower our craft that are more recognizable to our day-to-day lives. The important thing is to make it work for you, the one doing the magic.

If local animals do not appeal to you for a familiar, try doing the same type of reading and research on the natural environment of the animal that does appeal to you. If that animal is a leopard or a Komodo dragon, learn everything you can about their behaviour and habitats. Whatever animal you may be interested in, see how you feel about them after you have a more complete understanding of what they are really about. Do you still feel drawn to them when you know what they are really like, or do you prefer an idealized version of them? Just like any intimate relationship, it can have a "honeymoon" period. Are you still attracted once the filthy habits and weird quirks are revealed? An animal in spirit will still be that animal, warts and all.

Meeting the Animals in Spirit

Making first contact with an animal familiar is not as straightforward as going to a spirit pet shelter and picking one out and taking it home with you. The process is not happening here in our world; it happens in our dreams, in meditation, and when we take spirit journeys to the Underworld. Witches can use techniques such as journeying, divination, spellwork, and dream analysis to find their animal familiars. These techniques can open the door to the spirit realms where the animal spirits dwell and allow for the opportunity for a constructive meeting to take place. As much as you may want to attract a particular animal, the animal that comes through may be the one you need as opposed to the one you want. Allowing the right animal to come through and then accepting it allows you to learn something that spirit—and your subconscious—is trying to teach you. A witch's power comes from understanding their own power and potential. Our animal familiars can guide us into this learning by embodying aspects of ourselves in their archetypes and reflecting that back to us to learn from. I did want that great stag to reveal itself to me, but instead I got a polar bear. It revealed to me its true nature of endurance, patience, and strength through adversity—all things that I did not give myself any credit for but that I have to remind myself that I do possess. In fact, when I am being honest to my polar bear familiar, as well as myself, I excel at these things. An animal familiar's presence should empower the witch, strengthening their power and aiding when necessary. This relationship should be constructive, so if an animal comes to you that you did not expect, give it a chance to reveal its message and learn everything you can from it.

SPELL
Drawing an Animal Familiar

This spell is simple and requires only a few ingredients. The most precious ingredient is your time, as you will need to set aside ten to fifteen minutes per evening for seven consecutive days over a new moon. Consult your calendar to determine the day the new moon is on; this will be day four of your ritual cycle. Begin the process three days before and plan to end three days after the actual new moon.

Materials
- 1 teaspoon (5 ml) each of any three of the following dried herbs associated with dreamwork and astral travel: mugwort, chamomile, catnip, lemon balm, wormwood, yarrow, dittany of Crete, lavender
- 1 teaspoon (5 ml) frankincense
- A candle, preferably one made of a natural material such as beeswax
- Fireproof dish lined with sand or clean kitty litter
- Self-lighting charcoal (You will need at least seven discs.)
- Mortar & pestle (If you don't have this, crush the frankincense as finely as you can before mixing.)
- Small jar to hold incense mixture
- Lighter or matches

Directions
Add the three chosen herbs and the frankincense to your mortar and use the pestle to grind it until the mixture is well combined. Transfer this incense mixture to the jar.

Set up your ritual area with the candle, heatproof dish, self-lighting charcoal discs, and lighter or matches. You may also want to decorate your space with pictures, statues of animals, or found objects from nature. Make the space beautiful and make it yours.

On day one of your ritual cycle, light a charcoal disc in your dish. As it gains heat, relax and take three deep breaths. Allow the worries of the day to slip away and concentrate on the magic at hand. Focus on your desire to meet an animal familiar. When the coal is hot, light your candle and give it a moment to grow steady. When you are ready, place a generous pinch of your incense mixture on the charcoal and recite the following spell:

> **Beasts of the earth**
> **Flying creatures of air**
> **Swimmers in water**
> **I seek you; I dare!**
> **Be my familiar**
> **Reveal yourself to me**
> **This is my will**
> **So shall it be!**

Gaze into the incense smoke and allow your mind to wander. Do not force any thoughts or visions; just allow yourself to receive any thoughts or mental pictures that arise on their own.

When the smoke dissipates and you feel that you have taken the time you need, thank the spirits for the time you had together (even if you haven't seen them yet!) and blow out your candle. Write down any visions or spontaneous thoughts that came up. Repeat this process until day seven of the cycle. When the cycle is complete, review your experiences and notes for information on your animal familiar. The information you receive may be quite strong or very subtle. Do not overthink the images, sensations, visions, or intuitive messages you receive and bear in mind that the animal familiar may be very discreet or shy about making first contact with you. If you do not get a sense of an animal to form a relationship with, you can repeat this cycle at the next new moon.

Bonding with Your Animal Familiar

Once you have found your animal familiar, you are going to need to do some work to set up a relationship with them. In chapter 2, you read about how the relationships between people and familiars were defined in historical documents. In these examples, the common themes were that familiars in some way informed or taught their person, the relationships were usually kept private and intimate, and in some way the person would feed, give offerings, or sacrifice to the familiar. Looking at the available history provides some good ideas on the steps you can take in order to create a constructive relationship with your animal familiar and how to maintain it.

Ask for Information

Your animal familiar will need a job to do; this is the nature of the beast, so to speak. By reaching out to it for advice or information, you are enabling it to fulfill its purpose, and this will be rewarding for the familiar and for you too. The way you make your requests will depend on your personal style, and you may need to experiment to figure out what works best for you and the animal familiar. Some methods to consider are:

Divination

Using a form of divination that you are comfortable with, form a question in your mind, and then call upon your animal familiar to send you answers through the form of divination you have chosen. For example, if tarot is your divinatory method of choice, draw three cards and read those for the information you need.

Dreams

Before you go to sleep, spend a few moments in quiet meditation and ask your animal familiar to inform you through your dreams. Upon waking, try to write down any details of your dreams that you can remember. Do this over a few consecutive nights and pay attention to any patterns or unusual impressions you may recall.

Journeying

Chapter 5 includes a description of how to journey to experience the umwelt of an animal. You can use this technique to journey to the Underworld to meet your animal familiar and communicate with them.

Be Discreet

It may be very tempting to tell the world about your exciting, new animal familiar, but this may not serve you or your familiar very well. A witch's power is sometimes contained in silence, in keeping something private and discreet. In silence, we can really listen and hear the soft voices and gentle messages that we may miss if we are too busy talking or oversharing information.

Give Something in Return

Accused witches of the past were charged with feeding their own blood to their familiars, often by way of an extra nipple or witch's mark on their bodies. You may or may not have such a thing, but there are other ways to give back to your animal familiar.

Give Your Time

Set aside some regular time to focus on your relationship with your familiar. Add an element of ritual to this by lighting a candle, burning some incense, or just quietly meditating while holding them in your thoughts.

Lay Out an Offering

A simple bowl of water placed thoughtfully outside where physical animals can also enjoy it or set in a place of honour on your altar would be a good start. This could expand to include small servings of a food that the animal in physical form would enjoy, as this preference would extend to the spirit version of this animal.

Invite Them to Ritual

Don't forget to include your animal familiar the next time you do magic or hold a ritual. Light a candle for them or place a photo or figurine of what they would look like in physical form in your working space to represent them.

* * *

You have invited this animal of spirit into your life, and now you are responsible for the relationship that has started. Your animal familiar will stay with you so long as it is receiving something back from you. Like any relationship, you only get out of it what you put in.

Seeking an Animal Companion

The decision to bring a living animal into your life is a big one—that is, if you are taking the responsibility seriously. This creature will need food, water, and veterinary care. It may need training, and your patience will be tried. When it is old, it may face the same challenges that elder humans do—failing eyesight, deafness, sore joints, and long-term medication. Some animals, like parrots or turtles, may outlive us. I know an African gray guardian who has a care plan for their bird companion written into their will so that there will be no question of what to do when the human caregiver dies. These are the things we brush to the side when we get caught up in the excitement of adopting a new animal into our family; the newness and joy of bringing home a pet and potential animal companion is just too much fun.

The reasons for adopting an animal can vary from person to person and may change throughout a person's life. Young families may adopt a dog because they want their small children to have the experience of looking after a pet. Older adults may adopt an animal because they want a buddy to go for walks with or fill the void left when the kids move out, and single folks may just want another living thing to share space with so that they are not lonely. In most cases, we are hoping for the same ultimate cherished outcome—unconditional love.

It can be argued by any devoted pet guardian that they have some kind of reciprocal, loving relationship with their pet. A snake owner once commented to me that they loved the "hugs" their ball python would give them, even though they said that the constrictor may just have been measuring them to see if they could swallow them. That snake was most doted on, and the hugs were appreciated by both parties, in their own way.

When a witch adopts an animal, there may be a very specific cherished outcome—that the animal could become a magical companion and ally in their witchcraft practice. This is a tough one as these relationships demand that the animal has a natural inclination toward this sort of work and is willing to participate in its own way. This is just like working with other humans in that the activities must be consensual and comfortable for all parties involved to participate in. It is crucial to remember that there is no guarantee that the pet you adopt will be inclined to be your animal companion. You must be willing to accept that the adorable creature that you have just brought home may well remain a beloved pet for the duration of your relationship. It may very well grow into a magical working relationship, but it may not. There is also the possibility that your idea of what a magical relationship looks like will be challenged, and your beloved pet will develop into an animal companion on their terms, not yours. You may be the one who is learning the lessons that they have to teach you.

WORKING
Adoption Commitment Ritual

So, you have brought home your new pet and potential animal companion. You have thoughtfully considered all of your obligations and are now ready to state your intention to care for this creature to them and any deities, spirits of place, or powers of the directions that you feel compelled to evoke. Most importantly, you are affirming these commitments to yourself and pledging to see them through. In addition to this pledge, you will create a protective shield around your animal to form a cocoon of safety around them. If this animal will be going outside and being exposed to any number of risks, it will be especially helpful if they have some extra protection from harm.

If your pet is not the sort to sit still through a ritual, you can use an item to represent them instead. This could be anything from an appropriately shaped figurine to a stuffed animal, or you could try your hand at sculpting something out of self-hardening clay. Let your imagination guide you. You may want to cast a circle, but it is not necessary. If you are working with your actual pet, they may wander in and out of it anyway, so be prepared to be flexible.

Materials

- Your pet or item to represent them
- One white candle, preferably one made of a natural material such as beeswax
- Incense and an appropriate container to burn it in
- Moon water (see chapter 10) or plain water
- Lighter or matches

Preparation

Before you start, write your pledge. This can be a simple statement of intent detailing your commitment to take the best care possible of the animal you have adopted. You could say something like:

You are my pet, and I am your human
I will feed you and ensure you have fresh water
I will provide shelter and comfort to you
I will ensure you receive the best health care I can afford
I will exchange teaching with you, share my wisdom with you
And love you freely.
This is my pledge.

Directions

Start by setting up your ritual space, setting your candle and matches or lighter, incense and container for burning it in, and water on your altar or a table. If you are able to have your actual pet in the space, bring them close to the table. If not, set the item representing them on the table.

Create your sacred space by first inviting the powers of the directions to watch over and witness your ritual. Choose simple words that reflect your impressions of what the cardinal points of north, east, south, and west represent and how they relate to the animal you are doing this ritual to protect. For example, if the north represents the earthly realm to you, you could petition the Powers of Earth to grant you the ability to provide food and shelter for your pet. East may represent air to you, and you could ask for boons associated with thoughts and intelligence to make good decisions for their care. South may represent fire and the ability to take action quickly if there is a concern, and the west may be water, the emotional realm, where it is fitting to ask for the unconditional love we desire to flow freely between you and your animal.

Evoke any deities that you feel will be able to offer support and guidance to you and your pet. Refer to chapter 4 for some suggestions of which deities may be appropriate.

Ground yourself by taking a few long, deep breaths, and then connect with your animal by stroking them, gazing into their eyes, or holding the item that is representing them. Allow sweet, loving feelings to flow, and visualize you and your animal sharing a harmonious future together.

Light the incense and read your pledge out loud to your pet. Look at them, or the item that represents them, as you speak and take your time, allowing the wafting incense smoke to carry your words to the deities and directional powers you invited to be present.

Next, light the white candle. As the flame grows strong and steady, visualize the glowing light as a sphere, growing and increasing until it becomes a protective shield of energy that encircles your pet. Introduce your pet to this energetic protection, assuring them that this protection will help them stay safe and secure. When you can feel that the sphere is steady and stable, blow out the candle. Spend a few moments with your pet or the item representing them and enjoy sharing sacred space. When you are ready, thank the powers of the directions and the deities you invited for aiding you in the work and bid them farewell.

Keep the candle in a safe place and take it out and relight it periodically to reinforce the shield. You can also continue to do this throughout the pet's life, with or without the candle, by visualizing the shield as a glowing sphere of protection.

Meditative Touch

The animals that we share our homes with often appreciate the quality time we spend with them, and often this includes when we pet them, massaging their bodies, stroking their soft fur, or smoothing their feathers. Even snakes and other reptiles can enjoy sitting close to us, their cold blood being warmed by the radiant heat of our warm bodies. This intimate contact creates a bond between us and our companion animals and pets that we can mutually enjoy, each of us in our own ways, for the benefit of all those participating. This builds trust and sympathy between human and creature, allowing for a natural flow of energy that can be healing, energizing, and constructive.

Healing modalities such as massage and reiki are often appreciated by our animal companions or pets, but you don't need to learn either of these things in order to have some magical and bonding time with your animal friend. You just need to consider a few simple steps:

- Set aside a dedicated amount of time when you can focus completely on the animal—without any distractions. No mobile device, other conversation, or multitasking for the duration of this time. It is just you and the animal.

- Start by gently stroking their fur, feathers, or scales and gauge their reaction. Do they want to be touched? Are they leaning into it or moving to get away? If you are sure that the contact is being appreciated, continue. If you sense any reluctance, stop. This is about building a trusting relationship, not imposing your own agenda.

- Close your eyes and follow the energy of the moment as you run your fingers along the animal's body. Are there spots that are tense, hot, cold, or sensitive? Do they trust you enough to relax?

Older animals may have sore joints or muscles that may be soothed by this gentle attention, and younger animals can learn how to trust you through this quiet time together. In my own experience, this has helped me to understand when one of my pets, my cats or my dogs, have been having health problems, and it has also strengthened the bond and psychic connection between us.

When Oban was having problems with his liver due to the epilepsy medication he was on, he would tense up slightly when I ran my hands over his body near his liver. It gave me a clue that something was up. Because we had a regular habit of spending some quiet time together with me meditatively petting him, I knew how his body felt and what reactions were normal and which ones were not. I had experiences to compare, and this taught me a lot. He also would come to me for these meditative sessions, laying down beside me in a particular pose to say he wanted a session. It was our time together, and now, six years after his death, I can still clearly feel his fur and the shape of his body; this muscle memory brings me great comfort and helps me tremendously with the grief of losing him. Our veterinarian would remark that I had a sixth sense for detecting when a problem was arising with Oban, but it was keen observation and paying attention to quiet signals that made this happen. This is a lesson that Oban certainly taught me, and I carry that into my witchcraft. Small clues delivered quietly have great value to a vigilant witch.

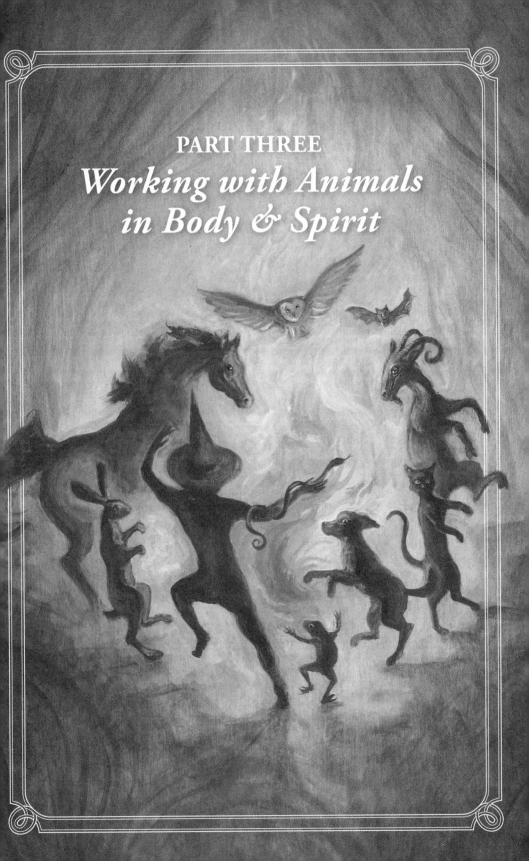

PART THREE
Working with Animals in Body & Spirit

CHAPTER EIGHT
A Witch's Toolbox & Animals

A witch's toolbox is usually loaded with crystals, stones, herbs, and spell ingredients for all sorts of human situations, but what about our pets and animal companions? In this chapter, I will discuss the use of some common things used in magic, how they can aid our animal helpers, and what risks they also pose. These lists are by no means exhaustive but can give you a place to start and base your own research off of.

One thing to remember is that the associations that a given magical item has in the physical world will also extend into the spirit world. If an item is helpful, healthy, and beneficial to a physical animal, that item will also benefit the spirit version of the same animal. If an item is dangerous or toxic to a physical animal, it will be equally destructive to the animal in spirit. There are a few exceptions to this rule, which will be noted in the chapter.

Safety First

It is vital to remember that not everything we do when we work our magic is safe for physical animals. A lit candle, smouldering incense, or anointing oil could be very dangerous, harmful, or even fatal. Please exercise caution when exposing animals to these elements of your activities.

Years ago, I lived with a very sweet but somewhat neurotic cat named Layla. She liked to be close to me, which was usually quite nice, but whenever I tried to burn a candle, Layla would manage to set her tail on fire or singe the hair along her sides, trying to rub herself on it. For safety's sake, I would banish her to another room and then have to listen to her meowing and scratching to be let out. As attracted as I was to the idea of Layla being my magical companion, she would remain a beloved pet. Needless to say, I did not burn many candles openly during her lifetime.

While I would have hoped that by some natural instinct Layla would have known that fire was a danger, I had to come to terms with the fact that she was just not able to understand that—not when it was coming from a candle, anyway. When introducing your pet or animal companion to the various elements of your witchcraft practice, take into account their aptitude and personality and the weird things they may be prone to doing that put them at risk.

Some pets and animal companions, such as dogs (but I have met cats and one parrot that do this), have the instinct to guard their homes against intruders. This can be problematic when you are hosting a ritual or gathering in your home where new people may overwhelm your defensive animal. Make sure you take time to properly introduce new faces to your animal before getting started. For the sake of everyone's comfort, you may want to sequester the household animals to another part of your home while your group activities are going on. For the comfort of the humans coming to visit, it is a good practice to inform or remind folks that you have animals in the house and that visitors with allergies should take precautions in order to have a comfortable visit. I usually have some antihistamines on hand for guests who may forget to come prepared.

Some pets and animal companions (and again, this is usually dogs) become confused and fearful when people they know wear costumes or masks that conceal their faces. They may be able to smell a friend, but the visual does not line up with the scent. Before donning ceremonial garb or masks, let your pets and animal companions sniff and examine any items that may confuse them. Oban would go absolutely insane if any of my male friends would put on a hat. I don't think he liked it when the familiar shape of their heads would suddenly change. As a result, hats were avoided or very carefully introduced to him.

Candles

As noted in the anecdote about my cat Layla, candles are an obvious danger to pets and animal companions. Cats may be a popular pet or companion for witches, but they do seem to be fixated on knocking things off of tables or jumping up on places where they do not belong. Candles are a highly effective and easily accessible magical tool, though, so it is worth locking the household animals out of your working space so that you can safely engage in some candle magic to commune with your animal familiar.

The flame of a candle is a liminal point that connects the physical world with the world of spirit. It is a common practice in witchcraft to light a candle when we evoke spirits or deities, as a place for their energy to focus while we do our ritual or magic. Spells will often include burning an object or piece of paper that has our intention projected or written onto it as a way to communicate to the spirit world the magical aid or goal we want to achieve. The flame is the transformational tool that transmits the message. These simple acts are powerful ones, and they do not involve anything more than a candle, a match or lighter, the item to be burned, and your will.

WORKING
Candle Communication with Animal Familiars

Candles can be used as a tool for maintaining and strengthening your connection to your animal familiar. The candle also provides a focal point for your contact with them, and the flame will act as a transmitter for sending and receiving messages with them. By designating a candle to be this focal point and returning to it on a regular basis, to light it, observe the flame, and be receptive to any intuitive message you receive or feel compelled to project, you will create a regular opportunity for contact with your animal familiar.

Materials
- Any candle of your choice large enough to burn for several hours, preferably made of a natural material such as beeswax; choose one in a colour that reminds you of your animal familiar.
- A candle holder appropriate to safely hold your candle
- Lighter or matches
- A drum, rattle, or percussive instrument (Clapping your hands works well if you don't have an instrument.)

Directions

Set your candle in its holder and place it on a table or other safe, flat working surface in front of you. Have your matches or lighter handy and your instrument with you. Spend a couple of quiet moments visualizing your animal familiar. Take up your instrument and play (or clap) a strong, steady beat. Visualize the beat drawing the attention of your animal familiar. When you get a sense that you have a connection with your familiar, put down the instrument and light the candle. Using your own words, tell your familiar that you are open and available to them whenever this flame is lit and that this flame is a beacon between their world and yours. Tell them of your commitment to light the beacon on a regular basis. Take some time to establish this connection while the candle burns. When you sense the connection fading, blow out your candle, bidding farewell until next time.

It is a good idea to have a backup candle to switch to when the one you are using burns down. Remember to light your new candle off of the burning end of the old one.

Crystals

Just as with humans, crystals can enhance the environment and well-being of an animal. Thoughtful placement of a crystal in a safe place near where the animal eats, sleeps, or is known to frequent can expose the animal to the benefits associated with that stone. There are many wonderful books and online resources available that detail the properties of crystals and their beneficial uses for humans, and these will also extend to our pets and animal companions.

If the animal you are working with wears a collar or a harness, you have the opportunity to attach a small crystal pendant or charm to it. This can be chosen for the benefit that you want to extend to the animal. If you have a cat that goes outside, you may want to adorn their collar with a small amethyst or moonstone, as both crystals are known as traveller's stones, offering protection and safe journeys to the wearer.

Crystals can be placed in dog- or birdhouses outside to give peace and comfort to the animals that live there or near nests in trees to provide protection for baby birds and their parents. If you have an animal that lives in a cage or a tank, the addition of a crystal would be an attractive decoration, as well as a source of potential metaphysical benefits, as long as you ensure that they can't hurt themselves on it.

Crystal Safety

Most animals will not be terribly interested in a crystal or rock in their environment, but caution should be taken with animals, particularly young ones that may be teething and need to chew, as they may be tempted to chew or swallow a small stone. The popular use of crystal elixirs—water infused with crystals, often in fancy water bottles designed for the purpose—may make it tempting to create some for your pets. If you want to give this a try, check first to make sure that the crystal you want to use is water safe. Some crystals, such as calcite, halite, and selenite, can dissolve in water. Mica can flake and fall apart, hematite will rust, and others may release toxins. For example, garnet and labradorite contain aluminium, and lapis lazuli contains sulfur. This is not a problem if you are wearing the stone as jewelry or enjoying its magical properties, but it is not a good idea for your pet (or you, for that matter) to chew on or lick these stones or consume any water they have been submerged in.

As mentioned before, the properties and benefits of crystals can be universally applied to all living creatures, but here is a brief guide to some that do have specific benefits to animals:

Crystal	Useful For
Amethyst	– Dispelling fear – Separation anxiety
Aventurine	– Recovery from abuse – Stress-related nerves – Relax animals in rescue
Black tourmaline	– Stress related to human contact – Conflict between animals in a household
Carnelian	– Lethargic or depressed animals – Low-energy or "fading" animals

Crystal	Useful For
Clear quartz	– All-around healing crystal – Boosts and amplifies other healing crystals
Hematite	– Grounding for animals (especially herd animals)
Moonstone	– Human-animal bonding
Moss agate	– Aids in keeping indoor animals in tune with the rhythms of nature
Petrified wood	– Skeletal issues and arthritis – Enhances security and sense of place
Peridot	– Confinement indoors or unnatural conditions – Jealousy
Rose quartz	– Aggressive behaviour – Stress and jealousy – Wariness of humans
Smokey quartz	– Transition to new home/environment – Shock – Stress and nervousness
Sugilite	– Death and dying

Essential Oils

In my own magical practice and mundane life, I use essential oils quite a bit. I love the powerful effect that scent has on both my conscious and unconscious mind, and I really enjoy the luxurious and exotic qualities these oils bring to my magical practice. I do, however, live with two dogs who have a much keener sense of smell than I do, so I try to remain cognizant of the fact that what may be a positive experience for me may not be good for them—and may even make them sick.

For magical and medicinal purposes, essential oils are my preference over fragrance oils. Essential oils are naturally occurring substances extracted from the fruit, leaf, blossom, wood, resin, or bark of a plant using either solvent extraction or steam distillation, while fragrance oils are not naturally occurring. They are manufactured using synthetic ingredients to imitate essential oils. The purpose of using essential oils in my spells and magical work is to invite the energy and spirit of the plant that the oil is from into the work I am doing. In this way, I am reaching out to the plant to collaborate with me and lend its properties to the work at hand. You just don't get the same connection or result when using a synthetic product. Even though essential oils are natural, this does not mean they are safe for animals to be in direct contact with.

Please note that there has been nowhere near enough conclusive research done on the safety of essential oil use on animals. In their pure, undiluted form, essential oils can be dangerous to animals, and they should only be used in diluted form—if at all. Even for humans, essential oils are usually diluted with a carrier oil before being directly applied to the skin. While there are all sorts of recipes out there for natural pet remedies that involve essential oils, they may not be safe for any animals, or they could just be safe for certain animals. For example, eucalyptus is considered safe for dogs but not for cats. A flea and tick repellant containing eucalyptus may be okay for your dog but dangerous for your cat. Read labels and be cautious.

In working magic, we sometimes want to use these oils to bless or anoint. Should your working present a situation where you would want to do this with an animal, the best solution is to use the most safe and sacred liquid of them all—pure, clean water. This water can be ritually consecrated for the purpose, or if you want something a little extra, you can use moon water. Chapter 10 has instructions for creating this.

For basic safety, here are some things to remember:

- Never try to get your animal to sniff an oil directly from the bottle. This can be overwhelming for creatures with a more acute sense of smell.

- Do not apply essential oils directly to the skin, fur, or feathers of an animal. They may try to lick it off and end up ingesting enough to make them sick, or worse.

- Do not feed essential oils to animals or add it to aquarium water. Even if it is an oil that is food safe for humans, it may be toxic to animals.

- If you have been handling essential oils, wash your hands before touching your pets.

- Consult with a trusted animal healthcare provider before using any essential oil-based product on your pet. Yes—this goes for any homemade natural pest repellents you may want to use as well.

- When using essential oils around animals—and this includes when using an oil diffuser—keep the area well ventilated, ensure that your pets can leave the area if they want to, and make sure you can take them outside or open a window if they appear to be in distress.

For reference, here are some popular oils that are toxic for dogs and cats, our most common household pets:

Toxic for Cats	
Cinnamon	Peppermint
Citrus	Pine
Clove	Sweet birch
Eucalyptus	Tea tree
Pennyroyal	Wintergreen

Toxic for Dogs	
Anise	Thyme
Clove	Juniper
Pennyroyal	Wintergreen
Pine	Yarrow
Tea tree	Ylang ylang

Herbs & Plants

The safest and most powerful plants you can use to aid animals are the plants that the animal in question would naturally eat. This ensures that the plant won't harm them, and it guarantees that it is a plant that will attract the attention of the animal. This may sound simple, but remember, it does not have to be complicated and fussy to be effective. Magic will take the path of least resistance, and the important thing is to have the satisfaction of knowing that your efforts are being rewarded with success. So, for example, if you are doing a spell for your horse, use hay. You could burn this as an offering or infuse water with it for anointing. For a cat, catnip is a natural choice, and for a rabbit, clover or carrot tops would work very well.

It may seem more obvious to say this, but it bears repeating—never feed herbs and plants to animals (or yourself) unless you are 100 percent sure that they are not poisonous or harmful in any way. Even when the herbs and plants are part of your witchcraft practice, they can still be toxic; magic does not negate this.

Animals will be curious around new and interesting smells, and they may want to investigate herbs and live plants that are potentially hazardous to them, so keep these things in a safe storage place and well out of reach from nosy pets and keep an eye out for any unusual behaviour. When my youngest dog, Georgia, was a puppy, she wanted to chew on everything, including any plant in the yard. This meant I had to make sure she wasn't chomping down on the monkshood or henbane that I have growing in my garden. It never occurred to me when I planted them that these witchy plants could be a danger to one of my dogs. After a couple of close calls, I had to fence off this part of the garden until she grew out of her teething stage. Common houseplants can also be toxic to pets, and cats especially have a tendency to nibble on the ones that can harm them.

We do use plant and other material in our witchcraft that can be dangerous for our pets and animal companions to eat or be exposed to, so be alert for any signs of unusual behaviour. An animal that has ingested or been in contact with something toxic may exhibit the following signs of poisoning:

- Drooling
- Muscle tremors
- Seizures
- Vomiting
- Difficulty breathing/irregular breathing
- Difficulty walking/staggering
- Redness or sores in mouth or on skin

If you see any of these signs, get them to a vet as quickly as possible. Inform the vet of the materials that you were working with so that they know what they are treating.

As with humans, herbs may be prescribed to an animal to help them with a medical problem. My dog Oban suffered from epilepsy and had to take medication for most of his life. One of the side effects of his meds was that it was very hard on his liver. His vet prescribed milk thistle capsules to support his liver function. This worked like a charm, and Oban was able to live a long life because of it. Please get the advice of a vet before treating an animal medically with herbs! Again, just because something is natural does not mean it is safe. Herbs are powerful and can harm as well as heal, and some herbs may also counteract the efficacy of other medications, so leave these decisions to the professionals. Herbs can be used safely in ritual or spells for effective magic to aid your pets without much risk as long as you remember that this should not replace proper veterinary care but support it.

The following table lists the magical properties of common herbs that should not cause your pet any harm if they should ingest a small amount. Do not attempt to feed any quantity to the animal, but instead use them for spells, incense, or charms.

Herb	Useful For
Bay (*Laurus nobilis*)	– Purification – Protection
Catnip (*Nepeta cataria*)	– Love – Psychic bonding
Chamomile (*Matricaria chamomilla*)	– Peace and calm – Antianxiety
Dandelion (*Taraxacum* spp.)	– Strength and energy (root) – Psychic connection and spirit communication (leaf)
Dill (*Anethum graveolens*)	– Protection – Luck

(NOTE: Use the herb form only; essential oil can be toxic to animals.)

Herb	Useful For
Hyssop (*Hyssopus officinalis*)	– Purification – Banishes negativity
Lavender (*Lavandula* spp.)	– Calming – Antianxiety
Lemon balm (*Melissa officinalis*)	– Love – Psychic development
Mint (*Mentha* spp.)	– Communication – Vitality – Prosperity
Parsley (*Petroselinum crispum*)	– Fertility – Protection
Rose (*Rosa* spp.)	– Domestic peace – Love and closeness
Stinging nettle (*Urtica dioica*)	– Protection *(NOTE: Use the dried form only as fresh stinging nettle can seriously irritate humans and animals alike!)*
Common sage (*Salvia officinalis*)	– Healing – Psychic protection
Turmeric (*Curcuma longa*)	– Vitality – Purification

Ritual Offerings: From Cakes to Kibble

A ritual offering is a devotional act to a deity, ancestor, or spirit. Witchcraft rituals often include offerings of food, alcohol, water, or ritual items that are laid out on an altar or shrine, either indoors or outside. Outdoor offerings can also be ceremonially laid outside in a special spot, such as under a tree or near a significant landmark, or they may be thrown into water. These offerings are usually made sincerely and with the very best of intentions, but sometimes they are made without considering the impact they are going to have on the natural environment or the animals that may encounter them.

Deities, spirits, or whatever non-corporeal beings that are being communed with do not usually fly down, pop up, or otherwise manifest and then literally eat or drink the offerings themselves. The consumption is usually performed by their emissaries—the birds, beasts, or insects that are native to the area. While the intent may be magical and devotional, the impact of the offering choices we make is most often felt by the living creatures in the environment, so it is really important for those of us leaving the offerings to make good, safe choices.

When my coven meets, we always save an oatcake and a sip of mead from our ritual feast to offer to our gods. When circle is over, two of my coven-mates have the responsibility to take these things outside and leave them under a designated tree. The mead is a small amount, maybe an ounce, and it gets poured directly on the earth where it is absorbed by the grass and ground. My dogs have figured out that if they follow my friends outside, the oatcake will be broken into two pieces so they, as the emissaries of our gods, can gobble up the offering on their behalf. The oatcakes are simple fare, wholesome and safe for dogs, and this way of offering makes the gods, witches, and dogs very happy indeed.

Safer Options

The safest and most universal ritual offering you can use anywhere, indoors or out, is pure, clean water. This may seem too simple, but it truly is essential to all life and a precious resource that can be appreciated safely and not cause harm.

If you feel strongly about leaving a food offering outside, give some serious consideration to what you choose. Start by thinking about the wildlife in your area, as they will be most likely to eat it. Is there something that you can offer that the wildlife will eat anyway? I live in an area with a lot of deer and a lot of apple trees. The deer eat the apples as part of their regular diet. Noticing this has led me to use apples as a staple offering item. They also have the added bonus of revealing a five-pointed star shape when they are cut across their equator, which really appeals to me and suits the witchcraft that I like to do.

Offerings to Avoid

Anything containing alcohol, caffeine, chocolate, sugar, or artificial sweeteners, xylitol in particular, should be ruled out. Processed or fast foods are not animal friendly at all and should be avoided. At best, these offerings will cause no real damage, but there is a possibility that they could lead to serious harm—anything from tummy upset to death—for the innocent creature that happens upon what appears to be an easy meal.

Offerings Indoors

If you are leaving your edible offerings in an indoor place, this is easier to control. You will just need to remember to leave it somewhere where your pets and animal companions can't get into it or leave out something that isn't harmful for them to dine on. Don't forget to remove the offerings before they rot or attract pests like mice and insects. Even a sacred offering is subject to the reality of spoilage and scavengers.

Nonedible Offerings

It is also common practice to leave nonfood offerings at outdoor locations. This could be something like a clootie, a scrap of cloth, or a ribbon that is tied to a tree branch with a wish or magical intention behind it. This seemingly innocent piece of folk magic can become harmful when plastic or synthetic fabric is used. It may be ingested by wildlife, causing illness and death, or it may become tangled in the wings or legs of birds or small animals, resulting in injury. These fabrics also do not decompose, and that magical intent becomes thoughtless litter and an environmental hazard. When presenting nonfood offerings, consider your magical footprint on the environment that we, as witches, should be advocates for. It is distressing to me when I enter a sacred place to find that someone has left plastic cups, aluminum tealight holders, or Styrofoam plates behind after a ritual or event. Do those responsible believe that the gods appreciate this environmental desecration? How could this possibly benefit the living creatures and spirits of these places? Being mindful of what we put into the natural world when we lay out offerings is one way that witches can be good stewards of the land that we should hold sacred.

Wielding Tools

The way we use the contents of our witch's toolbox is a reflection of our relationship with the world. Being thoughtless, inconsiderate, or dangerous with our tools can have a serious effect on the animals in our environment. With a bit of thought and consideration, we can instead build stronger and deeper relationships that will in turn reinforce our magic. I like to think of this like fine-tuning an old radio; it only takes a little extra focus to dial in a clearer, louder signal.

Time is also a tool, and spending some of your precious time in ritual or meditation with a pet, animal companion, or animal familiar is a bonding experience for both you and them. Animals of any realm love this attention equally.

CHAPTER NINE

Whiskers, Bones &
Other Animal Parts

Some of the most compelling and fascinating imagery associated with witch-craft includes the bones, teeth, claws, and fur of animals. Skulls from all kinds of creatures are found on sacred altars, jewelry made from everything from por-cupine quills to snail shells adorn devoted practitioners, and furs and hides are draped across the shoulders of witches, Heathens, and Druids alike. The close contact with these artefacts creates an aura of otherworldliness, of a simpler, more primitive time, when the old gods were more imminent and our ties with the natural world were yet to be broken, when human and animal were close family, and we wove our spirits together for survival and reverence with an atti-tude of respect. As we humans stepped further from our origins, attempting to become more civilized, and our mainstream religious focus became set above the natural world, we put our rough and wild animal garb down and picked up the refined cloth of the new religions of the world.

Witchcraft offers a return to working with animal parts and a reconnection with how the use of these things can put us in a state of communion and rever-ence with the natural world. This can be a divisive topic; not everyone is com-fortable with the idea of using pieces of what was once a living creature. Within my own circle of witch friends are folks who hunt to fill their freezer for the winter as well as strict vegans. The degree to which you choose to incorporate the use of animal parts into your own practice is a personal choice for you alone to make. Personally, I prefer to use naturally shed items, such as antlers, snake-skin, whiskers, and feathers, or found pieces from already deceased animals, such as shells or bones. I do not have what it takes to hunt. If my life depended

142 • Chapter Nine

on it, I would likely starve to death. I have found through experience that processing fleshy bones is a stinky, messy job that I can do, but I don't have the space, time, or fortitude to do it often. This is not an undertaking for the squeamish, but taking it on can be an act of reverence and respect for the spirit of the animal. It is an opportunity to put your own energy into the act of making the earthly remains of the creature ready for sacred work. For some, the sight of dead and decaying animals is incredibly distressing, and for others, bones, skins, and furs are just a normal, average part of life. The key is to be respectful and never wasteful or frivolous. As a witch and a human being, I see animals as equal living creatures that deserve the same dignity as I do.

Ethics and Laws

Before you begin to collect animal parts for any purpose, ritual or otherwise, it is strongly advised that you familiarize yourself with the laws in your area for obtaining, possessing, and selling animal parts. These laws can be very different from country to country, and within any given country, they may vary widely depending on which province, state, or territory you are in. In North America, for example, there are strict rules around how and who may be legally allowed to collect roadkill. In some areas you may require a permit, or you may need to be on a waiting list and registered with a government wildlife agency. It may also be considered poaching to remove the remains of dead animals or naturally shed parts, such as antlers, from a provincial, state, or national park. Even something that seems as innocent as picking up a feather from the ground and taking it home may be illegal depending on the species.

While laws may be very particular to a given region, there are two fairly international acts that inform local laws and regulations. Being familiar with these can help you make lawful decisions when collecting animal parts in the wild or purchasing them commercially:

- *Convention on International Trade in Endangered Species of Wild Flora and Fauna (CITES):* This international agreement, signed in 1973, covers most countries in the world. It was created to ensure that international trade of wild animals and plants is done legally and without threatening the survival of plants and animals in their natural habitats.[45]

- *Convention for the Protection of Migratory Birds in the United States and Canada:* This agreement, signed in 1916 by Canada and the United States, covers North America and was set in Canadian law as the Migratory Birds Convention Act. The US counterpart to this is the Migratory Bird Treaty Act. Under these acts, it is illegal to possess any part of most wild birds, including bones, eggs, nests, and feathers.[46]

* * *

Depending on what it is you are looking to collect, it may be possible to get a permit from your local wildlife agency in order to lawfully obtain that particular animal part. Consult directly with your local authorities for more information on this.

If you find yourself attracted to collecting restricted animal parts for using in your witchcraft, it is important to understand why. Is it the allure of doing something that is taboo, or do you sincerely believe that you absolutely require this bone, tooth, pelt, or feather for a genuine reason? Perhaps there is another way to get the same result using a different, legal ingredient.

Finding the Parts

The search for animal parts to use in ritual can be as simple as going online and looking for dealers who sell these things ready to use. You may even have a specialty shop in your area that sells bones, pelts, and parts. Taxidermy shops, fur trading and auction houses, and Indigenous handicraft suppliers are good places to check out when you come across them, but they can be hard to find depending on where you live. Antique shops and flea markets can be a fun and interesting way to hunt for these treasures. If you keep your eyes open, you can stumble upon bone specimens, mounted trophy heads, bearskin rugs, pelts, hides, or even bone-handled implements that you can repurpose into magical

---

45. "What is CITES?"
46. "Canada-US Convention Protecting Migratory Birds."

tools. A vintage fur coat can be remade into a winter cloak or a rug for your ritual space floor. A set of mounted antlers can be remade into a ritual headdress. Recycling antique animal parts is a respectful way to ensure that the spirit of the animal is honoured and their earthly remains are not wasted.

If you hunt or farm animals, you will likely have a ready supply of parts that you can process for magical purposes. If you don't fall into these categories, you may have to do a bit of research and digging to make connections with folks who do. You can try reaching out to vendors who sell meat at your local farmers market—they may actually raise and slaughter the animals themselves and may be willing to sell you the heads or bones of animals they have processed for meat. If you know of someone who hunts, they may be willing to part with skulls, antlers, or bones from their prey.

However you acquire your parts, there will be a process of cleaning, preparing, and using them for witchcraft, and I have listed some suggestions on the following pages.

Antlers and Horns

The great antlers of a stag are an evocative emblem, relatable to so many witches. The image of the antler is a sacred thing to so many of us who practice the craft. These bony appendages grow almost exclusively from the skull of male members of the Cervidae family, comprising of deer, moose, elk, and caribou. Female caribou, or reindeer, are the exception and will grow smaller versions of antlers. The antlers sprout annually, grow throughout the year, and then shed after mating season is well over. As the animal matures, the antlers will grow back larger and more elaborate over time. These are not to be confused with horns, which appear on animals in the Bovidae family, which includes cows, sheep, goats, antelope, and buffalo. Although similar in appearance, horns are not shed but continue to grow continuously throughout the animal's life and will appear on male and female animals almost equally.

Both antlers and horns have provided humans with material for making tools, weapons, utensils, jewelry, and art since prehistoric times. The allure of these materials continues to appeal to magical practitioners, and there is quite the demand for them to serve in our rituals and on our altars.

In North America, deer, moose, caribou, and elk are prolific. If you live in or near a rural landscape, you are likely to encounter at least one of these species, provided you are quiet and patient. In the city where I live, white-tailed deer have moved into my neighbourhood and make it impossible to garden much in my unfenced front yard. I occasionally come across a shed in the late autumn while walking in one of the local parks. These fallen antlers do not require much in the way of preparation or cleaning before being used for magical purposes—just some mild soap and water to remove any visible dirt or debris. Horn is harder to acquire as the animal would have to be dead in order to remove it from their skull, so for most purposes, a naturally shed antler would be preferable.

Do take caution if you are cutting antler or horn to make ritual tools or jewelry! Make sure to wear goggles to protect your eyes from flying dust and debris and wear a respirator to ensure that you don't inhale the fine dust that is produced by cutting and grinding tools, as this dust can seriously infect and irritate your lungs. The friction generated by cutting antler causes heat, and this leads to a nasty smell not unlike burning hair, so choose a well-ventilated place to do this work.

On a witch's altar, antlers and horns can represent the Divine Masculine, the god of the wild archetype, or a specific antlered deity, such as Cernunnos or Herne, or horned god, such as Pan. Pieces of antler or horn make excellent ritual knife or rattle handles, can be carved into fetish or charm objects, or crafted into jewelry. I was once gifted a pair of chunky caribou antlers that I turned into a few craft projects. Using a sharp handsaw and with the help of a carpenter friend, I sliced a section of antler into discs, polished them using fine sandpaper, and made a rune set as a special gift for a dear friend. Another section of the same antler fit so well into my hand it became the handle for a ritual tool. These items have particular significance thanks to our coven's association with antlered animals and the northern world of the caribou, not to mention all of the thought, work, and ritual that went into creating them. You just can't buy tools that hold the same meaning.

Feathers

The gentlest way of incorporating animal parts into your practice is to collect naturally shed feathers. Particularly in the spring, when birds are mating and nesting, it is pretty easy to find feathers lying on the ground. It is easy to forget that feathers can also carry mites or parasites that were living on the bird that they were shed from, so you should consider cleaning them before you bring them into your home. This is easy enough to do by placing the feathers into an airtight container with a couple of mothballs for at least twenty-four hours. Leave this container outside your home to avoid any pests getting inside and also to keep your pets safe from the mothballs. Once you have done this, soaking the feathers in a fifty-fifty mixture of isopropyl alcohol and hydrogen peroxide will eliminate most bacteria and viruses that the bird may have been carrying. This should be followed with a rinse in warm water with a bit of mild hand soap to remove any stubborn dirt and chemicals from the feathers, which can then be blotted dry with a towel and left to dry completely in a warm, sunny place or with a hair dryer set on a low heat, taking care to not distort the feathers' natural shape.

As part of a bird, feathers represent the element of air and communion with spirits and deities of the Upper World. They can aid in connecting with our higher selves, our thoughts, intellect and intuition, and psychic ability. Feathers can be placed on your altar to symbolize the element of air and whichever cardinal point you associate with it (some traditions place the element of air in the east, others place it in the north). They may be used to represent a particular deity. For example, a peacock feather could be placed on a devotional altar to the goddess Hera, as it was her sacred bird. They also make good ingredients in spells or charm bags, bringing their airy associations or the energy of the particular bird they are from to your magic.

The best feathers for magic are the ones you find in the wild, but it is important to remember that possessing certain feathers may be illegal, so it is advisable to consult with your local wildlife authorities to find out for sure.

Shells

As a child I was fascinated with shells. Growing up on the prairies, there were precious few opportunities to get close to a body of water that held any sort of shells, save for the occasional freshwater mussel shell along the riverbank of the Assiniboine, a leftover from a snacking gull. The iridescent interior of these shells would captivate me, and now, as an adult, the same sense of wonder washes over me when I find more exotic shells along the beaches of oceans or lakes. Shells are another relatively easy-to-find natural animal part that has many magical uses, and they can be fun to go hunting for. Shells, like rocks and stones, end up in the pockets of so many curious walkers; we humans can't resist these found objects. When collecting them in the wild, make sure that the shell is empty and not housing some small creature that should be left in peace.

Shells are the exoskeleton of the creature, which is to say it is the skeleton that is on the outside of the animal, providing support, protection, and structure. These seashells are not shed but continue to grow throughout the life of the creature. When we find them washed up on the beach, the inhabitant has died, and its flesh has either been eaten or naturally decomposed. To prepare shells for magical use, it is best to clean them thoroughly to remove any gunky organic matter and fishy smells. This is easily done by putting them in a bowl and covering them with hydrogen peroxide for a few hours, until you see a film forming on the surface. After this you can brush off any debris with an old toothbrush, rinse with clean water, and let them air dry. If you want to restore their natural lustre, rub them lightly with a bit of mineral oil. This process ensures that you won't have any nasty bacteria or nasty smells to contend with.

As part of aquatic creatures, shells not surprisingly represent the element of water and the emotional realm of feelings, dreams, and love, the tidal movements of the moon, and the mystery of the deep. They are powerful talismans on their own and make excellent bowls and saucers for holding spell ingredients on your altar. Large shells can serve as tealight holders or be lined with a generous layer of sand to serve as a charcoal incense burner. To connect with oceanic spirits and deities, you may want to set up a Sea Witch altar by using a large flat stone or piece of driftwood and decorating it with shells and found objects from walks along waterways in your area.

Snakeskin

Not all animal skins are the result of death. Snakes will freely shed their skin when they grow too large for their old one. They have the ability to grow a new, fresh layer of skin underneath the old one and then slither out of their old skin, freeing themselves from any parasites that may have latched on to their old form. This process, loaded with symbolism, is one that you can use to symbolize rebirth as well as transformation. These factors greatly inform the magical potential carried by the discarded skin and the symbol of the snake as a spirit capable of growing and reimagining itself continuously.

148 • Chapter Nine

If you find a snake shed in the wild, it is a good idea to wear gloves while handling it. Snakes may carry harmful bacteria, such as salmonella, so be careful and be sure to wash your hands and any surfaces that the shed touches.

Skins and Pelts

The use of animal skins and pelts has been part of human culture throughout history. Even today, with so many other nonanimal options available, we still adorn our bodies with the fur and flesh of animals. Skins and pelts are the outward appearance of a creature; the texture, colour, and character of the animal is often clearly distinguishable even long after it has been killed and processed. The fur industry has a lot to answer for in its cruel treatment of animals for this purpose and has made it difficult for people who live on the land and depend on traditional hunting and trapping practices in order to survive, to earn a living, and continue their cultural practices. For most of us urban or nonhunting witches, it is relatively simple to find vintage or recycled furs to use for most of our needs, and with a little effort and the wonders of the internet, you can source ethically harvested skins and pelts to use if that is something you feel compelled to do.

When we use the skins and pelts of animals for ritual purposes, we are inviting the spirits of those animals to be present and participate in our magic. Wearing a cloak made of fur or leather for ritual, for example, can evoke the spirit of that animal and can also draw the attention of deities associated with that animal. At the Autumn Equinox, my coven does the same ritual every year. As part of this, the high priest is dressed in a cloak that I made out of deer hide and wears an antlered headdress. Over the years, he has reported to me that as soon as the cloak is over his shoulders, or sometimes even when he just looks at it, he gets a sense of deer spirit energy and that he feels the presence of the antlered god it represents. This cloak has come to be a powerful connection to this deity with a magnetism and spirit that is tangible.

Recycled or ethically harvested furs and skins can be used to make a wide variety of magical tools, costumes, decorations, and instruments. They may take more maintenance and care than humanmade materials, but that extra bit of attention is worth it. Furs and leathers may need conditioning. Drums made with natural skins will need to be treated with oil or saddle soap and protected from extreme temperatures. Taking care of tools made from animal parts is an extension of the respect the animal should have had during its life, and in looking after the artefacts made of their bodies, we have the opportunity to build a respectful relationship with the animal in the spirit world. Looking at it this way can lead to a collaborative and constructive animal familiar relationship—if we make the effort to work these reverent acts into our witchcraft practice.

Bones and Skulls

The bones of an animal hold the life force, energy, and energetic signature of the creature they came from and are likely one of the most powerful and misunderstood items we use in witchcraft. The sight of bones in a ritual context can either compel or repel, depending on your attitude toward these things, even among Pagans and witches.

There are many ways to obtain bones, and some are more ethical than others. The bones of domestic animals, such as pigs, cows, and poultry, can often be purchased from your local butcher shop, and these can serve as good bones to practice bone processing and cleaning techniques on. Most witches I know are usually after more exotic or wild animal bones for ritual purposes, and these are often bones of animals that are animal familiars, mascots, or tutelary spirits to the witch or group of witches. These can be trickier to find and may involve searching the internet for a reputable seller of bones, reaching out to the wider community to find someone who legally hunts for these animals, or lucking into finding appropriate roadkill, which can be messy, problematic, and in many jurisdictions illegal. If you are willing to process a carcass and clean it for bones, you must accept that this is a long and involved process. Once obtained, fresh bones need to be defleshed, degreased, whitened, and dried. Small bones or teeth will need to be reattached, and you may need to repair cracks and breaks. If you have the fortitude for it, I have included basic instructions for processing bones at the end of this chapter.

Unlike the naturally shed animal parts we can work with, bones are the result of the animal's death, and we must not take this for granted. The bone is a direct link, connecting us to the very essence of the creature. It holds the DNA of the once-living beast and all of its ancestors and descendants, so treat it with reverence and respect, just as you would want your own remains handled. It is likely that the animal whose bone you are holding died in a traumatic way, killed by a hunter, a moving vehicle, or a fatal blow in a slaughterhouse. This energy will need to be cleansed, and the animal's spirit may need help being released to its afterlife, and I have included a ritual for this later in this chapter.

In ritual and on our altars, bones and skulls can remind us of our ancestors and our connections to the never-ending cycles of birth, death, and rebirth. They can provide a seat for our familiar animals to take when they join us for our rituals and celebrations, and they can serve as powerful protective amulets, guarding our homes and sacred spaces. Bones can represent the element of earth and the tangible realities of our lives, but they can also represent the fifth element: spirit. These associations may shift and change for you with the tides of the seasons and the work at hand.

If you are working with the bones of an animal you intend to honour as your animal familiar, you may want to show your reverence by "reddening" its skull. The red colour can be achieved through the application of red ochre, which can be purchased online or at an art supply store. To do this, make the ochre into a thick paste, using either red wine or water, apply it generously to the entire skull, and keep it damp by wrapping it carefully in plastic wrap. Allow it to sit for at least three nights; the nights before, of, and after the dark moon would be perfect for this. This allows the red colour, representing the life blood of the creature, to seep into the porous bone, symbolically giving it renewed life force and reanimating it as a sacred spirit ally. After it has sat for three nights, check to ensure that it has taken on a nice colour, then dust off the ochre, taking care not to wash it with water as this will damage the red stain. Give your reddened skull a place of honour in your sacred space and make sure to pay attention to it, making offerings of flowers, incense, or small natural found objects to show your respect and appreciation. This devotional act is a tribute to your animal familiar and is a tangible way to demonstrate your allegiance to them.

WORKING
Preparing Fresh Bones for Magic

There are a number of factors to consider if you are thinking about processing an animal carcass for its bones. The process can be quite lengthy depending on the size of the animal and the amount of flesh that is still intact when you start. It can be a really messy and smelly job, so you will need a large enough space with appropriate ventilation—ideally some outdoor space if possible. You may be able to get away with processing small carcasses indoors, but it is the smell that might be a real problem here. For these reasons, you may want to start small, with something the size of a mouse or squirrel, before taking on an entire deer carcass. Instead of going for a fully fleshed specimen, you can also try cleaning some raw bones individually first—or until you are comfortable with the process.

Step One: Cleaning

You may be lucky enough to find an already cleaned carcass in the wild. If the carcass is still quite fleshy, it is worth leaving it in a protected area outside and allowing nature to take its course. Smaller carcasses can be covered with an overturned bucket or plastic bin that is then weighed down to keep out scavengers and encourage insects to clean the bones for you. You may also consider burying the carcass, but this can be tricky as the weight of the soil can crush small bones, or you may even lose your carcass to scavengers who sniff it out and dig it up. I have successfully buried a mostly defleshed deer skull in a large plastic box filled with organic topsoil and compost, which I carefully covered and stowed away from prying scavengers under the front porch of my house. It took a year for insects and soil bacteria to clean the skull, and I did have to check on it periodically and spray some water on the soil to keep it damp, but this worked really well, and I was very pleased with the results.

Maceration is another cleaning technique that you can try, but it is more hands-on and messier than leaving bones outside or burying them. This process involves soaking the bones in water until the flesh lifts off of the bone. Use a very gentle, even heat over an extended period of time until all of the visible flesh has come off the bone. You can help things along by using a soft bristle brush to wipe away the stubborn bits. Do not try to rush the process by boiling the bones as this will cause damage to the bones and make the degreasing step much more difficult. Cold water maceration is a gentler option if you have a secure outdoor place to do it in, but it does take a lot longer—weeks or months depending on size. This involves submerging your bones in a bucket of water and weighing them down so they stay underwater. This can get really stinky as the bacteria from the carcass and the water work together to break down the soft tissue. You will need to check on the progress regularly and pour off the dislodged flesh and scummy water, leaving at least half of the water behind, and then top up the bucket again with unchlorinated water. Leaving half of the original water ensures that enough active bacteria remain and continue the work.

With all of the potential smell and mess that can occur with cleaning, letting nature do the work for you in a contained, secure space outdoors is my preferred method.

Step Two: Degrease the Bones

Even if your cleaned bones look white and clean, they still contain natural oils that will eventually come to the surface and cause the bones to turn yellow and appear greasy. To remove this oil, you will need to soak your bones in a mixture of warm water and dish detergent. The go-to and easy-to-find brand for this is usually Dawn, as it contains aggressive grease-busting agents that work really well. The process is straightforward: Place your bones in a bucket large enough for them to be generously covered with warm water. Add enough detergent to create bubbles, and then let this sit for a couple of days or until the water becomes cloudy. This is the grease lifting from the bones. Carefully pour the cloudy water down the drain; it is wise to place a colander in the sink when you do this so that any small bones are caught and don't end up going down the drain. Return the bones to the bucket, fill it up once again with warm water and dish detergent, and repeat this process until the water no longer turns cloudy. The number of times you will need to do this will depend on how much grease is in the bones. Be patient and make sure you are removing all of the grease before moving on to step 3.

Step Three: Whiten the Bones

For this step you will need a quantity of 3 percent hydrogen peroxide great enough to completely submerge your bones. I find that for this step it is best to find the smallest lidded container that you can fit all of your bones into where they can be completely submerged. For most bones you will want to soak them for at least twelve to twenty-four hours. Smaller, finer bones may not need so long, while large, dense bones may need to go a bit longer, so keep an eye on them.

Do not use bleach for whitening bones as it will destroy their structural integrity and ruin them.

Step Four: Drying the Bones

Now that your bones are clean, degreased, and whitened, you will have to remain patient just a while longer and let them dry out completely for at least a week depending on size. Lay them out in a well-ventilated, dry place, and turn them every couple of days so they can really air out.

Once they are completely dry, your bones are ready for witchcraft and magic. You may want to ritually bless them before putting them to work, and the following ritual may be your guide for this.

WORKING
A Ritual for Blessing Animal Parts

There is a strange separation that we humans have in how we categorize animals. Some are pets and family members, some are food, and some are so remote that we see them as distant objects. It can be easy to forget those leather shoes, that ritual drum skin, or the fur trim on a parka was once part of a living, breathing creature with its own intelligence and a heartbeat. How we each reconcile this, if we do at all, is a personal choice with no easy way for figuring it out.

What we can do as witches is choose how we honour the animal parts we use in our witchcraft. In order to prepare these parts for ritual and magical use, I suggest you start with recognizing the sacrifice of the creature and ensuring that its spirit is released to go wherever it needs to go to find its afterlife. Even if the animal died of natural causes, it may have been sick, hurt, or suffering before its life was over, and that may leave an energetic signature that may not serve your purposes either. By performing a ritual to release the individual animal's spirit and cleanse their body parts of the death-related trauma, you can begin to give the animal parts a new life as magical tools.

Tools
- The animal parts you want to work with
- A drum
- A handful of dried herbs for healing and purification (See chapter 8 for some suggestions.)
- Fireproof dish lined with sand or clean kitty litter
- Self-lighting charcoal
- Lighter or matches
- Photos or figurines of what the animal would have looked like alive

Directions
Before you begin, give some thought and do some research to the natural habitat of the animal in question. Make some notes about where they live, what they eat, and what their natural life cycle consists of.

Begin by setting up your ritual space, placing the animal parts, fireproof dish, herbs, and matches or lighter on your table or altar. Place the animal photos or figurines where you can easily see them and have your drum within easy reach. Next, meditate on the representation of the animal. This is what your animal parts looked like when they were alive. Close your eyes and place your hands on the animal parts, visualizing these parts as the whole animal again. When you have the image of the animal, alive and well, firmly in your mind's eye, pick up your drum.

Start drumming out a steady beat and let the nature of the animal lead you into how fast or slow this should be. A rabbit may be a quick, rapid beat, and a bear might lead a slower, heavier beat. As you drum, visualize the animal moving through the landscape that would be its natural home, eating, running, stretching, or doing whatever it should naturally do. Give thanks to this creature and enjoy the time you have together in this vision.

Drum for as long as you can comfortably hold the visualization. When it starts to fade, bid farewell to the animal and allow them to slip into their afterlife, released from any pain or trauma they may have endured. Slow your drumming and then stop, taking a moment for the experience of releasing the animal's spirit to sink in.

When you have taken in this moment completely, light the charcoal in the fireproof dish. When it is hot, place a generous pinch of the herbs on it, allowing the smoke to drift through your space. Pick up the animal parts and run them through the rising smoke to ritually cleanse and purify them. You may feel compelled to say words of gratitude or speak of the magic you plan to do with these parts. Ensure that every surface is exposed to the smoke.

When you are content that the parts have been completely cleansed and purified by the smoke, they are ready to begin their new lives as magical tools. Use them well.

A Sum of Its Parts

There is no doubt that animal parts have an evocative allure that really complements the atmosphere of witchcraft. Some of this is aesthetic, but there are very practical and purposeful reasons for this as well. When we choose to work with materials that come from the body of an animal, whether it was naturally shed or the result of an animal's death, we are, consciously or unconsciously, working in relationship with the spirit and energetic signature of that creature.

The key thing to remember is that they exist with us in the physical realm and the spiritual realm simultaneously.

In the material world, things are very straightforward. We can see the animals in their physical form, and we may care for them as pets or animal companions, or we may observe them as wild animals. We understand the parameters of these relationships.

In the spirit world, the dynamic changes and how precisely this realm works is a mystery, but it is apparent that this is a place where the animals can guide the relationships instead of us. When we pick up an animal part to use in our magic, we owe it to the original owner of that part to do so reverently and with great care and respect. What is true in the physical world is reflected into the spirit world. How we use and treat animal parts in this life will either create a positive working relationship with that animal's spirit, or it will create an unproductive one. The rituals we use to create positive relationships do not need to be difficult or complicated to be effective, but they do have to happen in order for that connection to be made.

CHAPTER TEN

Recipes & Rituals for Animals of Body

I am sure that I am not the only person who has loved a pet or animal companion and truly felt that in some magical way, that animal has taken care of me. The dogs I have lived with have barked to guard our house, my cats have been excellent snuggly nurses when I have been sick, and the wildlife outside my window provides daily entertainment and peaceful comfort. Without these animals sharing my life, things for me would be less interesting, lonelier, and lacking in richness and vibrancy. On every level, the physical animals in my life support my very existence.

I see these relationships as reciprocal. Just as we need them, sometimes it may be the animals that need our magic to aid them. You may have a need to perform a working to find a lost pet, offer protection to an animal, or heal a sick or wounded creature. Magical action combined with mundane practical care is how we can repay these beloved pets and animal companions for all they do for us. For example, to find a lost pet, you may want to do some divination to discover their location but do also report them missing to your local pet shelter and put up some missing posters too. A healing spell for an animal should support, not replace, appropriate veterinary care.

When you undertake magic on behalf of a physical animal, you are doing this based on your own perception of what may be right or good for this creature. Examine your motives. Are you trying to make their life better, or your own? Healing magic to prevent suffering and pain is generally thought to be a good thing, but is it good if it only prolongs the dying process into one that torments the animal? Think of the animal's best interest when working magic for them, as they cannot speak for themselves. A spell to ease their pain may end with the animal dying, a natural and transformational conclusion to all life, no matter how sad it makes us when those we love depart. As cute and sweet as baby animals are, a fertility spell for an animal will result in even more animals in shelters or, even worse, being euthanized. As with any magic we do as witches, we must weigh the consequences for taking these actions.

The spells, charms, and recipes in this chapter are meant to be guides and inspiration for your own creativity, and they are taken from my own practice and experience. If you don't have all of the materials that are suggested, follow your own witch instinct and find something that works for you. Enjoy the process and give yourself permission to be curious and experimental. Work with moon cycles but don't forget that witchcraft can be just as effective by daylight as well! Nature provides us with many opportunities to work with its tides and cycles; use and explore as many of these opportunities as you can. There are no "right" or "wrong" ways—but I would argue that there are more effective or less effective ways to do things based on your local landscape, natural resources, personal taste, traditions, culture, and disposition. You are the witch, and you are in charge of your own magic and power, so have fun and get your hands dirty making and doing magic.

RECIPE
Blessing the Beasts with Moon Water

All water is sacred. Water represents life, and it is also a basic need that all living things have in common. It is essential for survival, and it is a primary component of our bodies. Using water as part of a blessing is a common theme in religious practices around the world, which speaks to the universality of this simple yet powerful act.

The moon connects us with the mysterious, intuitive, and subconscious aspects of ourselves. We dream, reflect, and recharge under its influence. Many witches find that working in tune with the phases of the moon enhances and informs their magic, and this simple recipe is a good starting point.

Water is inherently receptive and may be programmed with the influence and intention that you direct at it. By exposing a vessel of plain water to the light of the full moon, you are collecting and storing its influence within the water.

Making a batch of moon water is an easy thing to do and it also does not have to cost any money, but you will have to invest some time, intent, and focus into it. As long as you are using clean, potable water, you can use this to safely anoint your pet or animal companion, and it is also safe for them to drink. You may want to make a larger batch and try using it for other magical purposes as well—to cleanse your sacred space, to water plants, to sprinkle outside as an offering to your local land spirits, or you can leave a small bowl of it on your altar as an offering to your animal familiar.

Materials
- 1 litre (1-quart) glass jar or jug, preferably with a lid
- Enough clean, drinkable water to fill the jar or jug
- Paint or markers to decorate your jar or jug with words or symbols to indicate your intention (optional)

Directions
On the night of the full moon, place your jar of water in a location where it can be exposed to the light of the moon, such as a windowsill or somewhere outside, and can remain undisturbed for the entire night. Speak out loud your intent to create moon water for the ritual of anointing and blessing the beasts. Spend a quiet moment visualizing this, and then leave the jar overnight. The moon water will be ready to use in the morning.

To use, wet your hands with the moon water and as you touch your animal gently and lovingly, say out loud to them something like:

I do bless you,
Creature of this earth
May you thrive, and never know
Hunger or thirst
Pain or neglect
Illness or injury

I am your companion
And you are mine
This is my word
So mote it be.

Store your moon water in a cool, dark place with the lid secured. You may want to top it up with additional clean water and repeat the process of leaving it out under the full moon every month so that you always have a supply on hand for when a need arises.

SPELL
Animal Protection Poppets

A poppet is a magical doll created as an effigy to represent the person or, in this case, animal that is the subject of the magic being worked. Creating a poppet to represent an animal that is important to you provides a focus for using sympathetic magic to shield and protect them from harm. Sympathetic magic works under the theory of "like attracts like." In other words, the actions and intentions you direct at the poppet will also manifest for the actual animal.

Before you begin, you will need to make or find a template of the animal shape you want to make a poppet of. You can either draw a simple animal shape on paper and cut it out or you can do a google image search for "animal shape template" or "(name of animal) shape template" and print it out. Make sure that your template is of an appropriate size so that you can cut two animal shapes out of your square of coloured fabric.

When selecting your stuffing material, try to use something that is easily relatable to the animal you are protecting. For example, if your animal sheds a lot of fur, consider brushing them out and collecting their fur to use. If you have a rabbit or guinea pig, use the wood shavings you would line their cage with. For a farm animal, use the straw that you would line their pen with. You can also use cotton batting, dried herbs or grasses, dryer lint, or anything you have on hand that would make a nice stuffed shape of your fabric animal body.

Choosing the embroidery floss presents yet another opportunity to layer in symbolism. I will sometimes use an embroidery floss colour to represent the type of magic I am working to "encircle" my poppet with, so for this protection poppet, I would use black thread, switching to pink if I was making a healing poppet or red if it was a love poppet.

Materials

- 30-centimeter (12-inch) square of coloured fabric (I prefer felt as it is easy to cut and will not fray.)
- Embroidery floss
- Darning needle
- Scissors
- Stuffing material
- Template in the shape of the animal you want to protect
- Pinch of naturally shed material from the animal you want to protect (fur, feathers, etc.)
- Protective herbs (See chapter 8 for suggestions.)
- Piece of black cloth
- Candle of any size, shape, and colour, preferably one made of a natural material such as beeswax
- Lighter or matches

Directions

Start by gathering together your materials; chose the fabric and embroidery floss in colours that represent your animal as closely as possible. Use your template to cut two animal shapes out of your coloured fabric. Thread your darning needle with a length of embroidery floss and use a blanket stitch to sew the two animal shapes together almost all the way around, leaving at least 1 to 1½ inches (2½ to 4 centimetres) of space open to insert your stuffing. Tuck your stuffing material into the animal body, including whatever naturally shed materials and protective herbs you are using. If you feel like being fancy, you can embellish your poppet with button eyes, add embroidery floss whiskers, or sew on some feathers for a bird. Be creative and personalize it however it suits you. Finish by sewing the poppet closed and tying off any loose ends.

To activate and charge your poppet, set aside approximately thirty minutes on a dark moon night. Place your poppet, piece of black cloth, and candle on your altar or table in front of you. Close your eyes and take three grounding breaths. Visualize your animal safe and protected from all harm. When you are ready, open your eyes and light the candle. Taking up the poppet, see it as your animal and say, "I recognize you as (name of animal)." Cradle the poppet in your hands and hold it carefully and safely above the burning candle. Say, "You are protected from harm." Next, place the poppet on the black cloth, and as you lovingly wrap the poppet up say, "You are wrapped in protection and comfort."

Blow out your candle and say, "So mote it be," and then tuck your wrapped poppet into a safe place in your home, such as a drawer or storage box, where it will not be interfered with or disturbed.

SPELL
Candle Spell to Attract Animals

This spell, like the poppet spell, is an example of sympathetic magic. This is a useful spell to do when you have made the decision to adopt a new pet and you want to attract the right one into your life, particularly if you have hopes of this pet developing into an animal companion that can be your ally in working magic.

The candle will represent you, and the symbols you carve into "you" represent the type of animal and your intention. For example, if your desire is to find the right horse to adopt, carve horseshoe symbols into the candle. For a bird, you may try carving symbols associated with air, where the bird flies.

This spell can be adapted to attract an animal familiar and not a physical animal if you prefer. If you go this route, be sure to carve symbols you associate with the spirit realm onto the candle so that your intent is very clearly stated. This could be as simple as actually carving the word *spirit* into the wax.

This spell is best performed under a full moon and should be performed over at least three consecutive nights.

Materials

- White pillar-style candle, preferably one made of a natural material such as beeswax
- Figurine or photo of the animal you want to attract into your life
- Tool for carving the candle, such as a burin, large darning needle, or nail

Directions

Start by holding the candle in your hands and charging it with your life force. You may want to blow on it and hold it over your heart to give it your breath and pulse. When you are ready, using your carving tool, begin carving the candle with symbols that represent the world of the animal you want to draw into your life. This does not need to be a work of art; your symbols can be simple shapes, letters, or numbers that you understand and that have significant meaning to you.

When your candle is prepared, place it in front of you on your altar or tabletop. Close your eyes and take three deep, grounding breaths. State out loud your intention to draw the animal into your life. When you have this intent clearly formed in your mind, open your eyes and light your candle. Take up your animal figurine or photo and hold it for a moment, visualizing the creature clearly, and imagine how that animal feels, sounds, and smells. Place the figurine or photo a couple of feet away from your burning candle. Let it sit there for a few moments, and then slowly inch it closer toward the candle. Let your intuition guide the path of the "animal." It may be a straight line, or it may loop around as you move it closer every few minutes. Do not try to force it; let the process of guiding the "animal" to the candle become a slow, meditative process, and allow your intuition to determine the path.

When you feel resistance or a loss of interest, stop the session, and resume on the following evening. State out loud your intention to resume the work at the same time the next day. By the third day, you should have your "animal" directly beside the candle. Take care to ensure that you do not accidentally ignite your photo if that is what you are using. If it is an animal in spirit that you are working for, check in to see how that connection feels. If it is a physical animal you are attracting, complement this spell with action in the world as well by checking in with pet rescues and shelters for adoptable animals or networking with friends for possible leads.

This spell, with a few tweaks, is also effective in drawing lost pets or animal companions back to you. The candle, representing you, becomes a beacon, guiding your lost animal home. Use a photo of your missing pet or animal companion or a figurine that represents them to intuitively inch them home. Be prepared that you may receive sad or confusing messages using this technique to find lost pets. I used this technique to try to locate my cat Louis when he went missing several years ago. I was immediately led to guiding the image of him directly to the candle. I was confused by this because after almost a week, he was still not home, and I was devastated and on the verge of giving up hope. It turned out that despite being lost, Louis *was* right beside me—he had somehow slipped into my next-door neighbours' house and gotten locked in the basement. Luckily my husband had delivered posters with his photo to all of the neighbours, so when Louis was discovered, it was easy for my neighbour to know whom to call.

RECIPE
Suet Cakes for Wild Birds

My late father-in-law was a bird guy. He built many birdhouses in his time, and he passed this love on to my husband, who devotedly feeds the birds that visit our yard all year long. I was only mildly interested at first but have grown to be fascinated by the movement of birds through our birdfeeders, and I love to get up early to drink my morning coffee and watch the birds swoop in for their breakfast. Of all the visiting birds, it is the woodpeckers who have stolen my heart. I have become increasingly obsessed with making sure I have something really good in the feeders for them. I learned about how woodpeckers need high-energy, easily digestible animal fat to keep warm, especially in winter, so I started to put suet cakes out for my woodpecker friends. As someone who likes to cook and experiment in the kitchen, I decided to make my own.

I live in a northern climate, so I like to make suet cakes around Samhain, when the natural food supply for local birds starts to run low. At this time of year, migratory birds also need the extra calories provided by the fat for their long journey to warmer destinations, and the birds that spend the winter along with the woodpeckers, such as nuthatches, chickadees, and blue jays, will also need the calories to survive the cold days ahead. These cakes can get messy and even go rancid if the outdoor temperature gets too warm (above 50 degrees Fahrenheit [10 degrees Celsius]), so they are best saved for those colder days.

I get bags of suet from my local butcher, and I shop for whatever raw, unsalted nuts or birdseed that is on sale. Adding in rolled oats helps the suet cake mixture stick together and hold its shape. Once finished, suet cakes should be stored in your freezer until needed outside. I recommend buying a suet cage from your local hardware or dollar store—they usually don't cost very much and are a tidy way to hang out your suet cake that is easy for the birds to land on and eat from. The cage also prevents the birds from getting the suet on their feathers and keeps both the bird and the suet safer from contaminants.

Equipment
- Medium-sized saucepan
- Mixing bowl
- Wooden spoon and/or rubber spatula
- 4 2½-gallon (9.5-liter) empty milk or juice cartons (Or any container that is of an appropriate size to serve as a mold to make a suet cake that will fit your suet cage or holder.)

Preparation
Make a suet cake mold by cutting down the carton to make a tray out of the bottom. My suet cage fits a cake that is about 5 x 5 x 1½ inches (13 x 13 x 4 centimetres)—so I leave about 2 inches (5 centimetres) off the sides of the carton.

Ingredients

- 1 pound (0.50 kg) suet
- 1 cup (250 ml) millet or mixed bird seed
- 1 cup (250 ml) unsalted raw seeds and nuts (Use shelled sunflowers, pumpkin seeds, peanuts, or whatever is on sale.)
- 1 cup (250 ml) quick-cooking oats

Directions

On low heat, melt the suet. Do not use high heat as suet is easy to scorch and is a fire hazard! Stir constantly and remove from heat as soon as all the suet is melted. Place the rest of the ingredients in a large mixing bowl. Once the fat has cooled slightly, gently pour it over the ingredients in the mixing bowl, stirring as you go. Once the mixture has cooled and thickened a bit, press it into your molds and leave them out to cool completely. Wrap them in plastic or waxed paper and store them in the freezer.

You may be tempted to try using other animal fats or vegetable fats instead of suet. The softer the fat, the easier it is for a bird to get accidentally covered in it, and this is dangerous for them. Greasy feathers do not insulate a bird from cold, and grease damages the natural waterproofing ability of feathers. Suet is safer because it tends to be drier and crumblier, which causes less risk for your feathered friends. Bacon fat or vegetable shortenings that contain salt, colour, or other chemicals are not safe for birds and should never be used.

When feeding time rolls around, pop a suet cake out of its mold and into your suet cage. Hang it outside from a tree branch or fencepost, high enough for the birds to find it and out of reach of pets. Saying a blessing over any food before you serve it imparts a sense of the sacred and makes any meal a special occasion. I like to say this blessing I wrote as I feed the birds:

Blessed be this food for thee
Oh little bird
May it nourish thee
As you fly so free

And high
Go feather your nest
And find it blessed
With your wee babes
a-fledging

RECIPE
Pumpkin Oat Dog Biscuits

Dogs love to eat, especially treats. The great thing about making your own homemade dog biscuits is that you know exactly what is in them, and you can add your own love and magical intent to the recipe. Pumpkin is a great source of fibre; it contains antioxidants as well as vitamins A, C, and E, plus minerals like iron and potassium. Pumpkin is also very good at settling a dog's upset tummy—I always have a can or two of pure pumpkin around for those times when one of my dogs shows signs of digestive upset. Apples also contain fibre, so dispense these treats in moderation! Overindulging in high-fibre treats, especially if this is a new thing for your dog, can cause diarrhea, so don't be tempted to overdo it.

Tools
- Food processor
- Large mixing bowl
- Small cookie scoop or a teaspoon
- Rubber spatula or wooden spoon
- Cookie sheet
- Parchment paper or silicone baking mat
- Fork

Ingredients
- 4 cups (1,000 ml) old-fashioned oats
- 1 apple, peeled, cored, and cut into chunks

- 1 egg
- 1 cup (250 ml) pure pumpkin puree (Not pumpkin pie filling—
  it has spices and additives that your dog does not need.)

Directions

Preheat oven to 400 degrees F (204 degrees Celsius).

Measure the oats into the bowl of your food processor and run it for about two or three minutes, or until the oats resemble chunky flour with some larger pieces remaining for texture. Add the apple and pulse until the apple is just blended with the flour.

Transfer the oat and apple mixture to the large mixing bowl. Add the pumpkin puree and egg. Stir until well combined.

Using a small cookie scoop or a teaspoon, drop rounded 1½-inch (4-cm) balls of the cookie dough onto a cookie sheet lined with parchment paper or a silicone mat. Flatten each ball with a fork or the back of your spoon.

Bake for twelve to fifteen minutes. Remove from oven and allow biscuits to cool completely before serving to your dog.

These biscuits will need to be refrigerated as they do not contain any preservatives. They keep for up to a week in the fridge. You may also want to pack some up in an airtight plastic bag and store in the freezer, where they are good for up to four months.

WORKING
Catnip Water Ritual

In the 1961 science fiction novel *Stranger in a Strange Land*, author Robert A. Heinlein tells the story of Valentine Michael Smith, a human raised on Mars.[47] Water is scarce on Mars, and when two people share this sacred resource they become profoundly bonded as "water brothers" (this term is used between any two people). This is where the popular blessing "may you never thirst" comes from, and this has become

---

47. Heinlein, *Stranger in a Strange Land*.

a common saying when sharing a cup of ritually blessed drink in neo-Pagan ceremonies.

My inspiration for this simple ritual came from my dear departed cat Roddy. I like to drink catnip tea, and when I would make it, Roddy would appear on the table, huffing the steam as it rose and then lapping up my tea, right out of the cup. Never thirst, Roddy.

For humans, catnip lowers fevers, reduces inflammation, aids digestion, and dispels gas. It is very good for calming anxiety, reducing stress, and encourages a restful night's sleep. For cats, catnip is an intoxicant, causing hyperactive behavior, zoomies, and frenzied playing followed by a lazy catnap—in most cats, anyway. Some felines do not seem to receive the wild side effects of catnip but appear to get the restful benefits. Offering catnip, dried or fresh, to your cat is a nice way of bonding with them as it is believed to create and enhance a psychic connection with them. Spending time together and sharing catnip, each in our own way, amplifies this benefit. It is also a bonus that by encouraging them to drink catnip tea, you are getting more water into their bodies, which is extremely beneficial, especially for older animals.

Catnip is part of the mint family and very easy to grow. It has more of a "grassy" taste, not the typical "minty" flavour. It can get invasive and quickly take over a garden, so corralling it in a pot may be a good idea. I have a large shrub-sized patch in a shady spot in my backyard. It does attract cats from around the neighbourhood, so if you grow some, be prepared for guests.

If you do not have a cat to bond with, this ritual can easily be adapted to suit any animal. The key is to have a liquid that you can share with them and that may be just plain water. My dogs love sharing chicken or beef broth, which is another option. You can also follow up by sharing a small snack as well after sharing water, adding a "never hunger" section to your ritual. A horse may like to have an apple you have taken a bite out of, or your gerbil may enjoy dining on a few seeds or nuts with you.

Tools
- Kettle or pot for boiling water
- Teapot

- Tea strainer
- Mug
- Small bowl

Ingredients
- 1 tablespoon (15 ml) dried catnip (Purchase catnip from an herb-alist or health food store if you can; the stuff you can buy from pet stores tends to be low quality and is not food grade.)
- 2 cups (500 ml) boiling water

Directions
Place the catnip in your teapot. Pour the boiling water over the catnip and allow it to steep for three to five minutes.

Strain 1 cup (250 ml) of the tea into your mug and strain ¼ cup (60 ml) of the tea into the small bowl for your cat. You may want to add some honey or lemon to your mug to taste. Make sure the bowl of tea cools to room temperature before offering it to your cat.

For the Ritual
Set aside at least thirty minutes to focus on your cat. Have the tea prepared and ready for both of you to drink. Encourage your cat to join you and make them the centre of your attention. If they won't stay with you, that is okay—let them wander as they need while you remain focused on them.

Set the bowl of cooled catnip tea down in front of your cat (if they have wandered away, set it down where they can find it). If they do not take to it right away, dip your fingers in the tea and let your cat sniff. Pet your cat with your wet fingers, letting them lick the tea from your hand and their fur. Sip your own mug of tea, allowing this to be a moment of shared experience together. Tell your cat things you want them to know, speaking out loud and focusing on your cat as you speak directly and calmly to them. Enjoy your time together, sharing tea, gentle words, and some good skritches. After you have had some time to enjoy each other's company, conclude the ritual by saying:

May you never hunger
May you never be cold, or alone
May your needs be met
May your body be strong, and healthy
May you have comfort
May we live together, content
(offer the bowl of tea, sip from your own mug)
May you never thirst

Give your cat one last good pet and state out loud that this ritual is concluded for now. The leftover tea can be kept in your refrigerator for up to five days. Cats tend to prefer room temperature food and drink, so when you pour some out at a later time, allow it to warm up before serving.

SPELL
Cat Whisker Charm Bag

It is no wonder that cats and witches have such a close bond. Cats do have the uncanny ability to beguile just about anyone, and the way they can stealthily negotiate through even the darkest of places and sense the world around them with their whiskers and paws is … magic.

The claws of a cat can be extremely sharp, and they grow continuously, much like our own fingernails. They use their claws for hunting, extra traction when they are running, and for self-defense. They will naturally shed the exterior layer of their claws, so you may find these outer layers, or claw sheaths, lying around your home. You may also be fortunate enough to find the occasional shed whisker lying around as well. These treasures make excellent ingredients for some highly effective charms, so gather these things when you find them, and then try your hand at using them to make magic.

A charm bag containing a cat's whisker can aid you with luck, balance, and negotiating your way through tight situations. Use this charm when you need feline grace to manage situations calling for stealth, dexterity, and the need to "land on your feet."

Materials

- One or more naturally shed cat whiskers
- A small cloth bag made of a natural, biodegradable material, 2-inch (5-centimeter) square is ideal
- A generous pinch of herbs associated with what you are making the charm bag for (See chapter 8 for suggestions.)
- Small pebble (Something found outside is perfect.)

Directions

Gather together the ingredients for your charm bag and prepare your ritual or working space according to your tradition or personal preference. This charm can be assembled whenever you need it, during any moon phase. In choosing herbs, make your selections based on the situation you need the charm for. Do you need luck, balance, and negotiation skills for managing a romantic relationship, medical situation, or a bad case of nerves? The chart of herbs and correspondences in chapter 8 may be able to help you.

When you are ready, begin to assemble the charm bag. Add the herbs first saying, "Powers of flora, aid my in my work." Next, add your small pebble and say, "Powers of earth, grant my will form and shape." Then finally add the whisker(s) and say, "Powers of the feline beast, cats great and small, empower this charm with your grace, balance, and skill!" You may want to add other feline traits here that suit your purpose.

Tie your charm bag closed and breathe on it. Your breath activates the charm and ties it to you. Carry it in a pocket or attach it to a cord you can wear around your neck and have it on your person as much as possible for the duration of the time you are dealing with the issue you created it for. When the need for the charm has passed, bury it in the earth or burn it.

SPELL
Cat Claw Bottle

Being scratched by a cat may cause *Bartonella henselae,* or cat scratch disease, a bacterial infection that causes swelling and lesions around the scratch site as well as fever, headache, and exhaustion. With all of this in mind, you can see why I recommend using shed claw sheaths in a spell to counter aggression that is being directed toward you.

Materials
- Small glass bottle with lid (A tiny one is actually more effective—it is more discreet!)
- One or more naturally shed cat claw sheaths
- Small sample of kitty litter (Work with used kitty litter if you can manage that.)
- Enough vinegar to fill your bottle
- One small yellow or green bead or crystal to represent a cat's eye
- Black candle, preferably one made of a natural material such as beeswax
- Lighter or matches
- A small black bag or scrap of cloth to wrap the bottle in

Directions
Gather together the ingredients for your spell bottle and prepare your ritual or working space according to your tradition or personal preference. I like to cast a circle and have my ingredients placed on my altar for this sort of work. I also like to work in tune with lunar cycles and would do this spell at the dark of the moon.

When you are ready, begin to assemble your bottle. Add the kitty litter first, saying, "Rest where you belong, and be aggressive to me no more." To this, add the bead or crystal, saying, "What you are doing shall be seen and revealed." Add the claw sheath third, saying, "You will be caught, as a cat catches her prey, and I will be released from your torment." Top up the bottle with vinegar and visualize your tormentor being caught like a mouse by a cat. Place the lid on your bottle and screw it down tight. Light the black candle and use the dripping wax to seal the bottle. Wrap up your bottle in the bag or cloth, saying, "No more shall you trouble me, as I will so mote it be!"

Discreetly slip this little package into the vicinity of your tormentor. For example, if they are a workplace bully, find a hidden spot near their workspace (I once buried one in an office plant pot near a tormentor's desk), or if it is a neighbour, roll it under a bush on their yard or tuck it into a hollow in a tree near their property. If it is not possible or safe to do this, bury or leave the bottle somewhere outside in the general direction of the person who has been tormenting you. After you place the bottle, walk away and don't look back.

On Equal Terms

For so many of us who practice witchcraft, we are forced to do so privately, often keeping this part of our lives a secret from our friends, family, and colleagues. It is not a given that we will be able to be openly and freely our authentic selves. Our pets and animal companions can be tremendous comfort and support in this, as they share our lives so intimately and do not judge us for what we believe in. The animals that we share our homes with are there beside us when we are being ourselves, uninhibited, and candid. It was when I realized this that I began to include my dog and cat companions in my thoughts, plans, and conversations about witchcraft and magic.

Spending quality time with pets and animal companions can include making eye contact; speaking directly to them as you would another human; preparing special food; focused sessions of grooming, cuddling, or touch; going outside for a walk—anything that allows for you both to acknowledge each other and that does not feel forced or coercive. Let the animal lead these moments together and allow yourself to enjoy the experience of being in the company of a living creature who sees you when you are truly yourself.

CHAPTER ELEVEN
Recipes & Rituals for Animals of Spirit

Working magic with animals in the spirit world gives you some creative license. You can use symbols, sounds, smells, and movement to convey your messages, to invoke and embody the spirit of the creature, and utilize your own intuition and power of visualization to engage with animal spirits. This type of witchcraft has a raw, primal energy about it, and you have the opportunity to leave your inhibitions behind and try things you may not usually do.

Folklore abounds with tales of witches who were able to shapeshift into animal form. In the guise of hares, cats, toads, or goats, witches were notorious for slipping into a nonhuman shape in order to go about their nefarious business. In these historic reports, the witch literally changed shape and possessed the abilities of the animal that they transformed into, running, climbing, or flying with animalistic grace and speed. Examining these accounts critically, we can only deduce that this was a metaphor for some other activity that the witch was actually engaged in. Much like the "flights" to the witch's sabbat, which were more likely to have been on the astral plane, we can assume that shapeshifting into animal form was a fantastic tale, misinterpreted from some true story.

Many people, and you may be one of them, report having dreams of being able to fly. Other folks I have spoken to say they dream of being able to breathe underwater and swim like a seal or otter. Ever since I was a small child, I have had a reoccurring dream in which I am able to run very fast, and then suddenly I drop down onto all fours and gallop at great speed, running like a wolf or bear through the woods, dodging trees, leaping over creeks and rocks, sure-footed and graceful, my animal body ripped with muscle and able to easily cover great distances. I have always woken up feeling content and peaceful from these dreams, and I carry a feeling of satisfaction with me for hours or even days afterwards. Could this be what shapeshifting feels like? I like to think so.

The closest I have come to recreating the feeling of shapeshifting that I experience while dreaming has been through the practice of ecstatic shapeshifting dance. Witches use movement and dance to raise energy and alter our state of consciousness. This often includes the addition of chanting, singing, or making music with drums, rattles, bells, or other instruments to heighten the experience. This can be an intimidating thing to attempt, and it is completely normal to feel self-conscious and awkward at first. I am the type of person who is not predisposed to dancing. I consider myself to be an awkward, clumsy sort of person, not the sort to dance under normal circumstances, so undertaking a shapeshifting dance was something I had to warm up to and ease myself into. It was so worth it, and I am glad I took that first leap of faith and gave it an honest try. I had the opportunity to attend some shamanic practitioner workshops that were led by two extremely kind and competent instructors who made me feel at ease and were able to create a comfortable atmosphere for experimentation with sound and movement. Once I was able to get out of my head and focus on the work, it felt much more comfortable and my self-consciousness faded. I did not have the initial success that the other participants in the class had, but I did eventually, after several attempts, have the sensation of connecting with animal energy that enabled me to move in ways I normally can't and see things I don't normally see. The experience did also leave me with a sense of satisfaction so like the feeling I would get after dreaming about running like an animal through the woods, and I loved being able to willfully recreate this while I was still awake, albeit in an altered state.

Another fascinating aspect of these experiences was being able to witness the dance and transformation of the other people in the room and the feeling of the atmosphere in our ritual space rising and changing as the drumming and dancing increased in intensity. I was able to see the otherworldly transformations on the faces of the dancers as they moved with their eyes closed, in a trace state, with movements that hinted at the animals they were shifting into. As shared as these moments were, we were all on our own journey, communing with our own animals.

WORKING:
A Shapeshifting Dance Ritual

For this ritual, you will need to plan a few things in advance. You can do this alone or with a group of people, so adjust these basic directions accordingly.

Start by selecting some appropriate music that you like. For this, instrumental music works best. Try to find a long track—at least fifteen to twenty minutes. A piece of music that starts slow, speeds up, and then slows down again is perfect. Try searching online for something atmospheric with a good backbeat. I have used the drumming tracks recorded by Howard Malpas with great success.[48] He offers tracks of various lengths, which is handy, allowing you to work up from a short dancing session of six minutes to a long session of thirty minutes. Have the music queued up and ready to play on your device of choice.

This ritual should be done at least a few times, and you will find that with practice it gets easier to fall into a light trance and shift into your animal. Do not give up or get frustrated if it takes a few tries to feel it! If you are like me and shy about dancing, it is worth experimenting on your own to get a feel for it before doing this with other people. Running through the music a few times so that you know when it is coming to an end will help you figure out when to start breaking away from your animal form and return to your normal human state.

Spend some time thinking about the animal you want to shift into. Study how they look and how they move. Are they quick or slow moving? Do they slither, run, or hop? Can they fly?

Once you settle on an animal, find something to wear that represents them. For example, if your chosen creature is a crow, you could wear black feathers in your hair or a black shawl to resemble crow wings. For a snake, you could wear form-fitting, slinky clothing or a snakeskin belt. This can be something small and symbolic or a full-blown costume; this is an opportunity to be creative.

---

48. Shamanic Drumming by Howard Malpas is available on Bandcamp: https://howardmalpas.bandcamp.com/album/shamanic-drumming.

Next, create a safe space for movement by clearing furniture and trip hazards out of your ritual space, ensuring you have appropriate room for yourself and any other dancers. Lower the lights and create ambiance for dancing unselfconsciously. Have a very simple altar laid out with basic tools on it, including candles and incense to help set the mood, and, if you are inclined, percussive musical instruments like drums or rattles.

Have some food prepared in advance to feast on after your dance ritual. This will help you ground yourself and return to your regular state of being. Dancing can be thirsty work, so setting out water and drinking glasses for all participants is a really good idea.

Begin the Dance

Open your ritual according to your tradition or what feels right to you. Greet the elements and invite any deities that are appropriate, such as your patron deities or deities that are associated with the animal or animals you and any other participants want to shift into. Light the candles and burn some incense.

Now that your sacred space is established, warm up your body by stretching and flexing your muscles. Take some time to breathe and check in with yourself. Give yourself permission to explore this ritual shapeshifting dance experience and the opportunities that it offers. Gently guide any other participants with verbal cues as you move through the ritual dance. When you are ready, press play on your device to start the music.

Visualize being outdoors in the habitat of your animal. Move around your space, allowing your body to move as the animal would move. If this feels awkward or uncomfortable at first, just relax and move in any way that feels comfortable, visualizing your animal as you go.

Maintain a clear focus on your animal and follow any messages for movement that you receive. Allow the animal's movements to become your movements and allow yourself to commune with the animal without overthinking or analyzing anything. Hop, flap, roll, or crawl if that is what your animal is guiding you to do. Continue moving until you sense the animal energy is dissipating or the music ends.

If your animal dance naturally ends before the music ends, step aside, sit down, and allow any other dancers in the space to continue dancing until the music ends. Continue to meditate on your animal if you can or take a moment to respectfully observe the movements of the other dancers.

When the music is over, take a moment to ground yourself. Check in with yourself and any other dancers and make sure everyone is content and back in human form before ending the ritual. Some folks may need a few extra moments to return to their normal state. If someone needs extra help, ask them to join you in taking three deep breaths. After the third breath, ask them to stretch their body, wiggle their fingers and toes, and tell you their name. Doing mundane things such as this is helpful in returning to a regular state of mind.

To end the ritual, say words of thanks and gratitude to the animal you connected with out loud and thank them for sharing their shape with you. Give thanks to the elements and deities you invited for joining you, then blow out the candles and extinguish the incense, declaring the ritual formally over. Have something to eat and drink.

Debriefing the Experience
Try not to discuss your experience with others for at least twenty-four hours. This will give you time to process what happened without the influence of what you hear other people say about their experience.

Dancing and experiencing the shift into an animalistic state is a technique that will help you build a closer sympathetic relationship with your animal. It may help to journal any insights or visions that you gain when you are dancing. It may also happen that you shift into the form of an animal other than the one you set out to shift into, so be prepared for the possibility that the animal that you want is not the animal that you need.

This way of interacting with animal spirits or energy is a form of communion and should be approached with a sense of respect and gratitude. It is a privilege to witness the transformation of other dancers, so please bear in mind that you are witnessing a very intimate thing, and do not laugh or tease another dancer for how they move during a shapeshifting dance; your words could be the reason they never attempt this magic again. This is a great opportunity to bolster and support the magic of others and, in doing so, your own magic as well.

RECIPES
Animal Spirit-Inspired Incense Blends

I have to admit, I am a complete sucker for incense. Nothing sets the mood for ritual more for me than the billowing of deeply scented incense smoke around my sacred space. Over the years, I have made it a custom to collect interesting herbs, resins, and essential oils whenever I can find them. When I travel and visit witch shops, herb or health food stores, farmer's markets, or apothecaries, I will take home these treasures as my souvenirs. I also like to grow many of my own herbs, and I dry them for culinary as well as magical purposes, such as blending my own incense.

For each of the following incense recipes, the tools will be the same. Self-igniting charcoal can be found at witch shops, church supply stores, or hookah supply shops. The heatproof dish can be anything that won't burn or melt. I like to use a terracotta plant pot saucer, which can be found at a hardware store or plant nursery. The sand or clean clay kitty litter acts as insulation from the heat. A mortar and pestle is a great tool to have on hand for any job that requires grinding herbs, resins, or spices.

Tools
- Teaspoon or small spoon
- Mortar and pestle
- Small jar
- Self-igniting charcoal
- Heatproof dish lined with sand or clean clay kitty litter
- Lighter or matches

I am terrible at accurately measuring out incense ingredients. I just use a teaspoon and eyeball that my parts are roughly equal. This is not rocket science! Just like any favourite recipe, your magical incenses will change over time and according to what you have on hand and your own personal preference. The teaspoon is a guide, not an absolute.

To mix each blend, the instructions are the same: Add the dried herbs and resin into your mortar. Grind and crush everything together with the pestle until the herbs and resin are well blended. Add in six to eight drops of essential oil gradually and continue to blend with the pestle as you go. The mixture should be slightly damp and a bit sticky. Transfer to a small jar for storage until you are ready to use it.

To burn the incense, place a layer of sand or clean kitty litter in your heatproof dish; this will absorb the heat and insulate whatever surface it is sitting on from being scorched. Light the charcoal and place it on the sand or kitty litter. When it is hot, add a generous pinch of the incense to the charcoal. Enjoy the smoke and top up as necessary.

Recipe: Shapeshifter Incense

This recipe is for when you want to create a smoke that will enhance rituals to journey to the realm of animal spirits or experience shapeshifting into animal form.

Ingredients
- 1 teaspoon (5 ml) of each yarrow, mugwort, and wormwood
- ½ teaspoon (2.5 ml) storax resin
- 6 to 8 drops patchouli essential oil

Recipe: Serpent Blend Incense

In many cultures and throughout time, serpents have been associated with the Underworld and seen as messengers, bringing the words of deities and spirits that dwell in those hidden places. This incense is for burning while performing divination or oracular work to encourage messages to come through from chthonic spirits and to aid in interpreting omens or signs from the Underworld. Best used for dark moon workings.

Ingredients
- 1 teaspoon (5 ml) cedar wood shavings (I recommend using the cedar wood shavings sold as bedding for rodents and chopping it up quite small and fine before you measure it.)
- ½ teaspoon (2.5 ml) ground clove
- 1 teaspoon (5 ml) dried rue
- ½ teaspoon (2.5 ml) dragon's blood resin
- 6 to 8 drops cinnamon essential oil

Recipe: Bird's-Eye View Incense

Try this blend when you want to fly to the Upper World to exchange messages with deities, spirits, or elemental forces of the air. It is very helpful for aiding you in making the distinction between your own sharp intuition and false messages or delusion.

Ingredients
- 1 teaspoon (5 ml) rosemary
- 1 teaspoon (5 ml) dried lavender buds
- ½ teaspoon (2.5 ml) copal resin
- 6 to 8 drops star anise essential oil

SPELL
Lucky Horseshoe

Hanging a horseshoe over your door or gate brings luck to all who enter through that portal. By painting and embellishing your horseshoe, you are adding your own magical intent to the item. It may take a bit of hunting to find an authentic horseshoe if you are an urban dweller like me, but it is worth the effort, and rooting through antique shops and flea markets is a fun way to pass time and find magical items.

Materials

- Horseshoe
- Fine sandpaper, about 150 grit
- Acrylic-based primer
- Acrylic-based paint, any colour you associate with luck (I like green or gold.)
- ½- or 1-inch (1- or 2.5-cm) paintbrush
- Ribbon and any other embellishments that represent luck
- Two small nails

Directions

Wash the horseshoe and leave it out to dry completely. Make sure there is no dirt or debris left on it. Prepare the surface by giving it a light sanding, removing any rust that may be on the surface. Wipe down the horseshoe to clean off any remaining dust. Apply a coat of the primer to one side of the horseshoe, making sure that all nooks and crannies get an even coat. Leave the horseshoe to dry completely, and then prime the other side. This step will ensure that your paint will adhere to the metal and not flake off. Repeat this process with the paint, doing one side at a time. Depending on the coverage you get, you may need to do an additional coat. When your horseshoe is completely dry, embellish to suit your personal taste and tradition. Horseshoes will have nail holes in them that you can weave ribbon through. You may want to paint sigils or symbols on your charm or tie on a bouquet for dried herbs or flowers associated with luck. The finished horseshoe can be hung by nailing it above a door or gate with the open end up or down according to your preference.

WORKING
Writing in Blood

The act of writing in blood is done to seal a pact and confirm your commitment to the magical deal you are making. Blood is life, and in using it for magic, you are giving this life to the cause your magic is for.

The act of drawing blood is not for everyone, nor is it always appropriate or necessary. Magic is an art that works with symbols, and blood can be symbolically represented by the colour red. Using red ink to seal a pact, write a spell, or draw magical symbols and sigils is a completely acceptable substitute for actual blood because it is the symbolism that conveys the important message.

It is possible to purchase commercial magical ink from occult shops and the like, but there is something to be said for making your own and imbuing it with your own passionate desire to do the work and see your magic through from start to finish. It is extremely satisfying to put effort into making your own magical tools and equipment, and this ink is no exception.

Both of the blood replacement inks in the following recipes use a resin called dragon's blood, a rich red pigment that comes from a number of exotic tree species such as the *Daemonorops draco*, native to Indonesia and Malaysia, and the *Dracaena draco*, which is of the Canary Islands. It can be expensive and hard to find, but a little goes a long way.

Once you have your ink prepared, you will need some appropriate paper to use it on. Your local art or craft stores will likely carry some nice parchment or thick watercolour paper, but in a pinch, any paper can work. A dip pen is an inexpensive investment, and I find these work best and clog the least when using homemade inks like these ones.

Tools

- Mortar and pestle
- Glass measuring cup, or similar nonporous vessel with a lip for easy pouring
- Small spoon for stirring
- Fine mesh strainer lined with a coffee filter
- Small glass bottle with a tight-fitting lid
- Dip pen

Directions

Place one of the resins in your mortar and use the pestle to carefully grind it until it is a smooth, fine powder. If you can purchase the resins in powder form, that will save you this step. Measure your powdered resin and transfer it into the measuring cup. Repeat with the other resins in the recipe. Give the powdered resins a stir to mix thoroughly. Then slowly add drops of the isopropyl alcohol (use at least 91 percent; the higher percent will dry faster) until the mixture becomes a smooth, slightly viscous liquid consistency. You want your ink to have some body and not be watery. Add one or two drops of the liquid indigo or blue food colouring if you want a darker colour. Add in a couple drops of the essential oil (for dove's blood, add a couple drops of pure vanilla extract—see recipe) and stir well. Strain out any debris by pouring the ink through the fine mesh strainer lined with the coffee filter, and then decant it into your bottle. Test it using your dip pen to ensure that you can write smoothly. Drop in one small clear quartz crystal to boost the magical intention of the ink. This crystal can be tiny; the size of a pea is perfect.

When not in use, keep the ink bottle tightly closed and store in a cool, dark place. If the ink becomes too thick, it will be because the alcohol is evaporating, and you can just carefully add a few more drops of alcohol to it to thin it out again. If you find that the alcohol is evaporating too fast, try adding a few drops of water to the mix. Always shake homemade ink well before using.

Recipe: Bat's Blood Ink

While there is lore out there that tells of witches using actual bat blood in spells, that is not really necessary, and no bats need to be harmed in order for this ink to be highly effective in your spellwork. Bat populations are in great enough danger from diseases such as white-nose syndrome, which is responsible for killing millions of the creatures across North America. They don't need to be hunted for their blood. Bat's blood ink is effective in the writing of spells or drawing of sigils that are for baneful or malevolent magic, the breaking of hexes, or magic to protect from serious harm.

Ingredients

- 1 tablespoon (15 ml) dragon's blood resin powder
- 1 tablespoon (15 ml) gum arabic powder
- Half part myrrh resin powder
- Isopropyl alcohol
- 2 drops cinnamon essential oil
- Liquid indigo or blue food colouring
- Small clear quartz crystal

Recipe: Dove's Blood Ink

The dove is more than just a bird; it is a universal symbol of peace, hope, and compassion. Many species of doves are known to mate for life, making them also a symbol of everlasting love and commitment. Dove's blood ink is recommended for writing spells or drawing symbols and sigils for magic related to love, healing, peace, and benevolent causes.

Ingredients

- 1 tablespoon (15 ml) dragon's blood resin powder
- 1 tablespoon (15 ml) gum arabic powder
- Isopropyl alcohol
- 2 drops rose essential oil
- 2 drops pure vanilla extract
- Liquid indigo or blue food colouring
- Small clear quartz crystal

Using Magical Ink

Each of these inks can be used for their general intended purpose in combination with your own creativity and will. The presence of the bat or dove spirit energy adds an extra layer of symbolism to your spell, as does the colour, fragrance, and ingredients of these inks. These are all tools to aid you in the magical work you set out to do.

Start with small batches of ink; you can always make more as needed.

Working: A Simple Spell with Magical Ink

Begin by setting your intention and deciding whether you need bat's blood ink or dove's blood ink based on the descriptions of their purposes I have provided with the recipes.

Tools

- The ink of your choice
- Dip pen
- Paper (parchment, watercolour, or paper of choice), approximately 4 x 6 inches (10 x 15 centimetres)
- Lighter or matches
- Large fireproof bowl
- Pitcher of water or fire extinguisher

Directions

Arrange your items in front of you on a table or desk. Ensure that you have at least thirty minutes of time when you are sure you will be undisturbed. Meditate on the subject of the spell you are about to do. What is your goal? Visualize it as clearly as possible and hold the image of your desired outcome as clear and strong as possible as you complete the remaining steps.

When you have that image firmly in your mind, begin to compose the words of your spell in your head. Keep it short—no more than four sentences. When you are ready, write the words of your spell on your paper using your dip pen and magic ink. Form the letters of each word slowly and carefully, holding the image of your desired outcome in your mind as you write. Do not worry about punctuation or grammar. You may want to write this in the form of a short poem or rhyme, or you may simply write down exactly what you want in brief descriptive sentences. Do not get hung up on the word structure or form; just pour your intention and will into the act of writing your words down.

When you are done, take a moment to appreciate the work that went into what you just did. The effort to find and acquire the ink-making supplies, the paper, and the dip pen. The effort to grind the resins and mix the ingredients. The power of this spell has been brewing ever since the first moment that you decided to apply your will and create the ink. The cumulative energy of all of your actions have been building for this moment. As the ink dries on the page, visualize the words of your spell truly sinking in and these actions building the power.

When the ink is dry and you are ready, pick up your spell paper, fold it in half, then half again. Place it into the fireproof bowl and set it on fire using your lighter or matches, saying these words:

Red is the blood, red is my fiery will
May all that is written here, be real and appear
(*if using bat's blood ink*) Under the moon, on bat's wings
(*if using dove's blood ink*) Beneath the sun, on dove's wings
May my desire be carried on the wind, to be fulfilled
This is my will, so mote it be!

Allow the paper to burn down to ashes. When the flame has gone out and the ashes and bowl are cool enough to touch, take the bowl outside and gather the ashes in your dominant hand. Close your eyes and visualize your cherished outcome one last time, then open your eyes and blow the ashes from your hand, allowing them to scatter to the wind. Turn around and walk away without looking back.

The Magic We Make with Animal Spirits

Working with animal spirit energy presents us with the challenge of acting on impulses and using our bodies and creativity in ways that we need our instinct, intuition, and gut to experience. It can, at times, be difficult to find the words to describe our experiences because our culture and society usually does not teach or share these things. Dancing as an animal or using symbolic blood to convey messages is not something that is openly discussed in most places. These actions do create a sense of otherworldliness, a time and place apart from mundane reality and a gateway into the world of the animal spirit energy that can aid and enhance the magic you may feel drawn to explore. I encourage you to give these things a try and follow your own intuition to find what helps you connect to the rhythm and flow of the animal spirit energy that resonates with you.

CHAPTER TWELVE
Saying Goodbye

The death of a beloved pet or animal companion can be one of the most profound losses we can experience. I can say with complete conviction that I have never grieved harder than I did when Oban died. This grief was the consequence of the love and multilayered relationship we had for almost sixteen years. In those darkest moments, I could not imagine ever having a pet or animal companion ever again. Looking back, I can see how that anguish eased gradually into accepting the reality that I am, truly, a dog person. There were homeless dogs out there that needed someone, and I am happier when I have a canine companion to share my life with.

Six months after Oban's death, we welcomed Lola into our home, and a new chapter was being written. Four years later, a tiny puppy, Georgia, came to live with us, and the joy of raising a baby animal and watching her grow eclipsed the fear and dread of the inevitable loss that I know will someday occur.

When we take an animal into our homes, we do so knowing—whether we acknowledge it like this or not—that their lives are shorter than ours and that they will likely predecease us. Even with this hanging over our heads, we still adopt these creatures into our lives and homes because the experience of living with animals is so worth it. The joy and companionship they unconditionally offer us overrides the concern about the sadness we will experience when they die. Human beings seem to have the remarkable ability to forget pain and try again. By the same mystery that we are able to fall in love again after a painful breakup, we allow new animals into our lives even after the death of a deeply loved animal companion or pet has shaken and hurt us.

Rainbow Bridge

Where do our pets and animal companions go when they die? We have theories and beliefs about what happens after death for ourselves, but how does this relate to the animals we live with? A particular vision of a pet afterlife was proposed in the book *Beautiful Joe's Paradise* by Margaret Marshall Saunders. This book, published in 1902, speaks of a lush green meadow with abundant food and water and healing from pain and mistreatment, a place where the animals' spirits travel by hot-air balloon to rest, rejuvenate, and await the arrival of their humans' spirits so that they can move on to heaven together. The popular poem "Rainbow Bridge" introduced the idea of a rainbow as the means by which the spirits of the animals and their humans could cross into heaven together. The origin of this piece of writing is a bit murky, and there are many versions of it floating around on the internet, on sympathy cards, and on posters often found hanging in veterinarians' offices. In every version the idea is the same—when we die, the spirits of deceased pets and beloved animals will be waiting for us at the Rainbow Bridge, where we will have an ecstatic reunion with them before crossing the bridge together and continuing on to heaven:

> Just this side of heaven is a place called Rainbow Bridge.
>
> When an animal dies that has been especially close to someone here, that pet goes to Rainbow Bridge. There are meadows and hills for all of our special friends so they can run and play together. There is plenty of food, water and sunshine, and our friends are warm and comfortable.
>
> All the animals who had been ill and old are restored to health and vigor. Those who were hurt or maimed are made whole and strong again, just as we remember them in our dreams of days and times gone by. The animals are happy and content, except for one small thing; they each miss someone very special to them, who had to be left behind.
>
> They all run and play together, but the day comes when one suddenly stops and looks into the distance. His bright eyes are intent. His eager body quivers. Suddenly he begins to run from the group, flying over the green grass, his legs carrying him faster and faster.

You have been spotted, and when you and your special friend finally meet, you cling together in joyous reunion, never to be parted again. The happy kisses rain upon your face; your hands again caress the beloved head, and you look once more into the trusting eyes of your pet, so long gone from your life but never absent from your heart.

Then you cross Rainbow Bridge together.[49]

This version is credited to Paul C. Dahm, a grief counselor. A rhyming version of the poem was written by Steve and Diane Bodofsky in 1998 that also captures the same themes.

As much as I admit to taking some small comfort in the idea of such a green and lovely paradise for animals' spirits to rest in when they die, I struggle with the idea of these beloved animals waiting around for us to die so that they can continue on to heaven. I like to think that all creatures have individual destinies to fulfill and that an animal should be considered in the same way that a human may be for an independent afterlife—on their own terms.

As a nonbeliever in the idea of heaven (or hell for that matter), I have to imagine that there are alternatives for those of us who believe in other versions of the afterlife. As a Wiccan, I look to my tradition to provide me with a belief system that helps me manage and cope with death. Years ago, when I was still seeking my spiritual path, I read *The Meaning of Witchcraft* by Gerald B. Gardner, and it gave me the hook I needed to seek Wicca on a deeper level. He wrote:

> They considered it good that men should dance and be happy, and that this worship and initiation was necessary for obtaining a favourable place in the After-World, and a reincarnation into your own tribe again, among those who you loved and who loved you, and that you would remember, know, and love them again.[50]

This idea really spoke to me as I immediately related what Gardner was describing to experiences I have had. I have occasionally met people for the first time and really felt that I did indeed "recognize" them as if we had known each

---

49. "Rainbow Bridge Poem."
50. Gardner, *The Meaning of Witchcraft*, 25.

other all of our lives. One of my coven-mates and I shared this feeling when we were first introduced at a Beltane event in our hometown more than twenty-five years ago, and we still reflect on how profound that meeting, or rather, our remeeting, was. We mutually agree that we recognized each other that day, and we have been very dear and close friends in this life ever since. It feels liked we just picked up where we left off in our last incarnation. This recognition was exactly what struck me the first time I laid eyes on Oban, and it was what propelled me to do whatever I had to do to adopt him and bring him home. It is what motivated me to take the very best care of him that I possibly could. It is the promise of our eventual reunion that comforted me when I was so lost to the depths of grief when he died. My experiences have made me believe in a type of reincarnation that applies to all life forms and that pets and animal companions are included in this. As hard as death can be to cope with when it happens to someone that you love, my tradition, Wicca, has provided me with a coping mechanism that suits me down to the ground and the flexibility to understand that it may not be the same for everyone.

However we may view the potential for an afterlife, it can feel like a small consolation in the moment that our beloved animal dies. The deep grief and sadness can be excruciating, and this pain comes from the shock of the loss and a feeling of emptiness and powerlessness.

Coping with Grief

When Oban died, I could not look at the gaping hole that his absence made in my life. I had to stay busy, and I was clearly overcompensating by doing unusual and sometimes destructive things. I went back to work the next day, pretending nothing was wrong, but went out on a break and smoked my first cigarette in years. I gathered up all of his stuffed toys and obsessively would smell them, his sweet doggy scent would bring him back to me with jarring clarity. Our daily walks together were my special time with him that I used to decompress and relax. I could not face being alone, walking down the sidewalk or to a park, but I forced myself to go for walks anyway, just short ones at first. I had no idea how to walk down the street without his leash in my hand, so I ended up treating myself to ice cream so that I at least had a mission and something to hold as I wandered along, figuring out how to be in the world without him.

When a beloved pet or animal companion dies, it can feel more devastating than losing an important human from our lives. Realizing this can often leave us feeling conflicted or guilty about the depth of our grief, and this can make us do things to hide how we are truly feeling. The last thing we need to hear is that our recently deceased pet or companion was "just an animal" or that we can "go get another one" from the usually well-intentioned people who are trying to console us. In these dark moments of grief and loss, it will be crucial to try to remember that how we grieve is a completely individual experience. There is no hierarchy for who should receive more or less of our grief when they die. The number of tears shed will be the right amount for how we feel about any particular loss, and when the time to grieve the loss of an important animal comes, be patient with yourself and honour those feelings. This may be a time to lean into your witchcraft practice and tools for aid. You can try some of these things to give you focus:

- **Create a memorial altar to your beloved pet or animal companion.** On a shelf, table, or area on a desk or counter, set up a focal point for honouring their life. Decorate this space with photos of the animal and items they may have played with or worn. A favourite toy and their collar, for example, would work really well. Then add an offering bowl so you can lay out token amounts of their favourite treats or water. This can give you some comforting continuity as you transition away from their daily care. Add a candle to your altar and take time to light it when you feel sad and want a moment of meditation with the memory of your animal.

- **Own your power and your feelings.** If someone asks you how you are doing, try to be as honest as possible and let them know that you are grieving. Opening up can give the other person an opportunity to offer support and express their own memories of a beloved animal. If they do not understand or brush off your pain, just tell them firmly that you are not looking for advice or feedback but that you would appreciate their patience at this difficult time. Generally speaking, our cultures and societies do not do well to understand the deep relationships that can happen with pets and animal companions, and it is not your job to try to convert an unsympathetic person while you are grieving. Accept genuine support when it is offered, but do not allow unsympathetic people to make you feel worse.

- **Work through your grief.** Suppressing your grief and sweeping it under the rug will not make you feel better, and it may cause further trauma. Grief hits our body, mind, and spirit, so remember to look after your physical, emotional, and spiritual needs as you go through the process of coming to terms with the death of your pet or animal companion. Eat, sleep, hydrate, exercise, and maintain your spiritual and witchcraft practices. Your beloved pet or animal companion thrived when you did these things with them, and you need to continue to thrive despite your grief. Your animals will benefit from you continuing to work magic with and for them as they transition into the spirit realm.

- **What is remembered lives.** Embrace the memories of the time you spent with your animal. Use your power of visualization to recall the wonderful experiences that you shared and use these images to comfort and sustain yourself. Speak their name out loud and share stories about them whenever you can so that you may celebrate them and all that they meant to you.

I went through a period after Oban died when I desperately wanted him to remain with me as my animal familiar. I guess I assumed he would, and I became frantic when I could not automatically locate him in the spirit world. This was something that I had to work through very carefully and pragmatically. He was a creature in his own right, with his own umwelt and sense of being. I have come to understand that this means that his spirit also had its own journey to take upon his death. Of course there is no way of confirming, measuring, or truly knowing the mystery of where the life force energy or spirit of anyone goes when they die, but if I extend my own dearly held belief in reincarnation to Oban, I can only assume he has moved on to his next life, whatever and wherever that may be. I can only trust that when my time to cross the veil comes and I learn the mystery of death that I will be fortunate enough to be reborn into a place and time where I can meet, recognize, and love Oban again.

WORKING

A Ceremony to Celebrate the Life of an Animal Companion or Pet

In the depths of grief and sadness, taking some kind of action can be an effective way to regain some sense of control and purpose. Expressing this in a ritualized way can be extremely helpful for your healing process.

An effective way to manage this grief is to take control of the situation and do something that alleviates the pain and gives you a way to express how much the life of your pet or animal companion meant to you. Creating a memorial ritual can be a powerful and effective way to gain some closure and perspective. Treat this as you would a funeral service for a deceased human and consider inviting family members and friends who also had relationships with the animal. Dress in clothing that expresses your mourning, in all black for example, in the clothing you would wear to take them for a walk or muck out their stall, or in clothing that still has their hair all over it. When your ritual is over, put out food and drink for yourself and any guests and have a wake or memorial feast. If it is practical to include foods that your animal would have enjoyed, do so, and eat it joyously in their honour.

Materials
- Taper candle (Try to find one in a colour that reminds you of the animal.)
- Candleholder
- Plate or dish to set the candle on
- Sand or salt, enough to cover the plate
- Burin, white-handled knife, or large nail to carve the candle
- Box of tissues, for the inevitable tears

Directions
Take the candle in your hands and hold it gently. Take note of how it feels as you allow yourself to honour the love and fond memories you have for the animal. If other people are participating, give everyone a

turn to hold the candle and reflect on their own feelings and memories. Using the burin or other implement, carve the name of the animal into the candle. Carve additional words or symbols that convey your affection and feelings for them. Secure the candle into the candleholder and place the candle and holder onto the plate. Spread enough sand or salt on the plate to cover it in a generous layer. This will catch any dripping wax, and you can also sprinkle flower petals or herbs on it or write messages in it. Breathe deeply and visualize the animal as you remember them at their best. Light the candle and say out loud:

> **Horned Lord of the Wild Places**
> *(Name of animal)* **has left this world and**
> **is crossing the veil between this life and the next.**
> **Guide them on their way**
> **Soothe them in this transition and aid them should they need it**
> **Give them peace, free from pain or harm.**
> **Let them be free and joyful.**
> **You who knows the mysteries of birth, life, death, and rebirth,**
> **Give comfort to** *(name of animal)* **and we who mourn them.**
> **May** *(name of animal)* **rest, renew, and**
> **be reborn among those who love them!**
> **In your name, Horned One, so mote it be.**

Allow the candle to burn for as long as you need to reflect and reminisce. Invite other participants to contribute their memories. Write words or symbols in the sand or salt on the plate as messages to your animal. When you have taken the time you need for now, blow out the candle. Lay out and partake of the memorial feast, sharing happy stories and memories of the animal.

Return to light the candle every day until it has burned right down. As the candle burns down, visualize your familiar animal moving peacefully into their own afterlife, free from pain or discomfort, happy and free. When the candle has burned down as far as it can go, collect the candle stump, the sand or salt, and any herbs you may have added into a biodegradable container, such as a paper bag, and either bury it outside or, if you can, burn it ritually.

Putting in the Time and Effort

Rituals, spells, and magical acts are rewarding ways to honour the animals in a witch's life, but there is still more that you can do. All of that magic can become quite hollow if that is where your relationship with the pets, animal companions, and animal familiars in your life begins and ends. Finding ways to extend your commitment into your daily life in the mundane world can be equally rewarding.

Reverence is often displayed through sacrifice, and that word is rather loaded. While it is true that *sacrifice* can mean the ritualized killing of a living thing, it does have other meanings that are more constructive. To sacrifice also means to give up or surrender something precious in order to further a cause you believe in. For so many of us in this hectic and busy world, the most precious commodity we have is our time. To sacrifice your time to a cause that creates a better world for animals is an act of reverence to the creatures we love and, by extension, to the spirits and deities that they are connected with.

Just about anywhere you go, you will find animal shelters in need of capable people to help care for the animals they rescue. The animals need to be fed and watered, the enclosures need to be cleaned, and vet bills need to be paid. Your time, or your money if you can spare it, will greatly help the frontline folks doing this work. Often animals are in need of foster homes, a temporary place to land while they wait for forever homes to take them in and permanently adopt them. Giving back to the animal kingdom in these ways can be as beneficial and life-affirming to you as it is for the animals.

Taking care of animals in the wild can be equally rewarding. My husband manages watering stations for the abundant wildlife that passes through our property. As soon as the snow melts and the risk of ice has passed, he lays out various sizes of bowls and birdbaths filled with fresh water for the deer, chipmunks, squirrels, rabbits, raccoons, and birds that live in the neighbourhood. He keeps them clean and free of debris so that anyone needing water can get their fill. A small sacrifice of his time and effort can make a huge difference to a thirsty creature.

For those of us who eat meat, it can be worth the extra effort to learn about where that food came from and how the animals were treated before they were slaughtered. All meat consumption comes from an animal that has been killed, but it can be argued that not all animal farming practices are equal and that some are indeed far less humane than others. By avoiding meat products that come from big-business, intensive animal farming operations, you are saying no to animal farming operations that are exceptionally cruel to the animals and also to the environment. In our crowded and increasingly urban world, this is difficult to do if you still want to consume meat, but it is worth thinking about and implementing as much as your reality allows. For me, this has meant increasing the number of vegetarian meals I prepare and saving meat for occasional consumption. As much as I do try to return to a full-time vegetarian diet, I still have hard cravings for meat, beef in particular, so I try to be as careful and conscious about my choices as possible.

Giving Thanks

In whatever way you choose to ritualize, honour, make sacrifice, or make better decisions in dealing with the animals in your magic or mundane life, be grateful. Say thank you to your pets when they do something positive, lay offerings to your animal familiars when they aid your magic, and bless the meat on your table before you eat it. Blessing food makes eating it a sacred act. By taking the time to recognize the value of this gift, we can come to appreciate the value of the life that was taken so that we may eat. Try using these words to bless the meat or animal products you consume and see how it affects your attitude toward eating it:

> **In the name of the Lord of Animals, the protector of beasts**
> **I do bless this offering of meat**
> **May this gift sustain me and those I share it with**
> **May we grow stronger and healthier with its aid**
> **We shall not waste or take for granted**
> **This most sacred offering**
> **To the creature who laid down its life, we are thankful.**
> **Hail the animals!**

We are on this earth together with so many creatures, seen and unseen. Sharing the planet in as harmonious a way as possible brings a better quality of life to all of us.

Conclusion

The COVID pandemic provided most of the world with a period of great hibernation. It was a time when I, like millions of other people, was forced into seclusion, away from the world I had known and into a world of introversion, meditation, and reflection. The wider world was closed for business, and as the pandemic unfolded, we were induced to reinvent ourselves and find new ways to live. Sequestered at home and unable to gather together in groups, I, like so many others, took comfort in doing domestic things, such as cooking and crafting, and also in spending as much time as possible outside, going for walks with my dogs around the neighbourhood, exploring parks and the long stretches of bush and forest along the river near my house. I began to see the hidden gift that this pandemic was offering me and my witchcraft practice, a gift that came wrapped in quiet and stillness.

I was able to hear sounds that I had never registered before. The pandemic-inspired lockdown had grounded planes and reduced vehicle traffic on the ground, making birdsong sound louder. I could hear the chittering of chipmunks clearly, the whickering of the deer that would come through my front yard, their hooves clip-clopping on the driveway as they passed my bedroom window, and the rustling of the colony of bunnies that moved in under the juniper bush in the front yard. The introversion of humanity and the dimming of our noise left room for the wild creatures to come out, emboldened by the reduced din of us humans. I truly felt that I was really seeing and especially hearing these creatures clearly for the first time. It was as if a key that had been ever so slowly turning in a lock finally clicked and a door swung open, revealing to me a very different version of my environment, one where the singing of birds and harrumphing of raccoons told little stories about things that my life before had drowned out.

Concurrent with these revelations, I was doing research for another creative project that had me diving into witchcraft history, reading about the people who were persecuted for allegedly practicing witchcraft. So many of the documents from this period contained details of the relationships the accused had with animals as familiars and as co-conspirators in the sinister activities the condemned were believed to be involved in. I could see how some of these themes have echoed down through the ages, becoming the cliché and often tacky, cartoonish stereotypes of witches and their familiars that we see today. Looking around me at this humming world of animal behavior that was bustling around my home, I wondered where the kernels of truth were and how the folklore of the past could be useful and practical to the reality of modern witchcraft practitioners today. How did the demonic animal-shaped imps of folklore relate to the "fur babies" we celebrate today?

When we practice witchcraft, we crave contact and communion with the hidden realms, to travel beyond the limits of our physical bodies and have experiences that empower us to create effective change to our mundane reality. I believe that in order to do extraordinary things, we need extraordinary allies. The non-human beings that exist beside us could be those allies, but in order to create those relationships, we must not overlook them. We modern witches are easily drawn to the flash and allure of the fantastic, the extreme, or the Hollywood version of what our craft might be and less observant of the quieter, less visible magics of the animals that live in our homes or in the wild around us. It is my hope that this book has provided some insight into the umwelten of the animals that you encounter every day so that you may pause and respect them for their unique intelligence and the abilities. I challenge you to slow down and visualize what their perspective may be able to teach you and hope that these quiet lessons empower you to work great magic.

It brings me great comfort and inspiration to know that there are colours, sounds, and smells all around me right now that I cannot perceive but that my dogs can. It keeps me humble to know that the tiny indigo bunting nesting in the hedgerow near my house in Winnipeg has migrated all the way from Florida, flying by night and navigating by the stars, something I could never manage. I am in awe of the snapping turtles in the river who overwinter in the mud, below the ice and brutal cold of a frozen plain. Learning these things and taking these lessons into my witchcraft connects me with these secret worlds, these real and true worlds, where the animals guide me. My beloved dog Oban was my first patient teacher in these things, and in the quiet days of the pandemic, the wild things offered their lessons to anyone who chose to listen.

Anyone who has ever had a deep connection with an animal, moments of psychic connection or intuition with a nonhuman creature, can surely agree that this is the "talking animal" of folklore and fairy tale. The dreamer who has been able to fly like a bird or run like a wolf in their sleep-world has certainly known what it is like to shapeshift. The witch who has danced and chanted in sacred space and allowed an animal spirit to enter their body, stepping aside to give this spirit reign over their human form, is in relationship with their animal familiar. When we incorporate these things into our witchcraft, we step into our power, away from self-consciousness, away from what is correct and civilized, and closer to discovering the truths of how we can be in harmony with the divinity inherent in nature. We do these things to learn, we do these things because we are curious, and we do these things to affirm our connection to the natural world because we want to remember that there is magic—and we are a part of it.

Bibliography

"1604: 1 James 1 c.12: An Act against Conjuration, Witchcraft and Dealing with Evil and Wicked Spirits." The Statutes Project: Putting Historic British Law Online. Accessed February 26, 2023. https://statutes.org.uk/site/the-statutes/seventeenth-century/1604-1-james-1-c-12-an-act-against-witchcraft/.

Aburrow, Yvonne. *Auguries and Omens: The Magical Lore of Birds*. Chieveley, England: Capall Bann Publishing, 1994.

Baldwin, William. *Beware the Cat*. London, 1584. Accessed May 26, 2023. https://www.presscom.co.uk/halliwell/baldwin/baldwin_1584_en.html.

Bekoff, Marc. *The Emotional Lives of Animals: A Leading Scientist Explores Animal Joy, Sorrow, and Empathy—Why They Matter*. Novato, CA: New World Library, 2007.

Bernard, Richard. *A Guide to Grand-Jury Men*. Internet Archive. https://archive.org/details/AGuideToGrandIuryMen. First published in London, 1627. Printed by Felix Kingston for Ed. Blackmore.

Brumm, Adam, Adhi Agus Oktaviana, Basran Burhan, Budianto Hakim, Rustan Lebe, Jian-Xin Zhao, Priyatno Hadi Sulistyarto et al. "Oldest Cave Art Found in Sulawesi." *Science Advances* 7, no. 3 (January 2021). https://doi.org/10.1126/sciadv.abd4648.

"Canada-US Convention Protecting Migratory Birds." Government of Canada. Updated September 2, 2022. https://www.canada.ca/en/environment-climate-change/corporate/international-affairs/partnerships-countries-regions/north-america/canada-united-states-protecting-migratory-birds.html.

Cocceianus, Cassius Dio. *The Histories of Rome*. Book LXII.

Clottes, Jean. "The Lascaux Cave Paintings." Bradshaw Foundation. Accessed August 10, 2023. https://www.bradshawfoundation.com/lascaux/.

da Silva, Sara Graça, and Jamshid J. Tehrani. "Comparative Phylogenetic Analyses Uncover the Ancient Roots of Indo-European Folktales." *Royal Society Open Science* 3 (January 2016). https://doi.org/10.1098/rsos.150645.

Dante, Alighieri. *Inferno*. Cantao XXIV. 1308–1320. https://www.fulltextarchive.com/book/dante-s-inferno/3/#CANTO-34-1.

Davis, Nicola. "Pole Position: Human Body Might Be Able to Pick Up on Earth's Magnetic Field." *The Guardian*. March 18, 2019. https://www.theguardian.com/science/2019/mar/18/humans-earth-magnetic-field-magnetoreception.

de Grummond, Nancy T. "Haruspicy and Augury: Sources and Procedures." In *The Etruscan World*. Edited by Jean MacIntosh Turfa. Abingdon, England: Routledge, 2013. Routledge Handbooks Online. https://www.routledgehandbooks.com/doi/10.4324/9780203526965.ch26.

Ermacora, Davide. "The Comparative Milk-Sucking Reptile." *Anthropozoologica* 51, no. 1 (June 2017): 59–81. https://doi.org/10.5252/az2017n1a6.

Fleming, Rev. Abraham. *A Strange and Terrible Wunder*. London: University of London. Accessed May 23, 2023. https://pure.royalholloway.ac.uk/ws/portalfiles/portal/4386955/Straunge_and_Terrible_Wunder.pdf.

Gerald, Gardner B. *The Meaning of Witchcraft*. Lake Toxaway, NC: Mercury Publishing, 1999.

Gooley, Tristan. *The Lost Art of Reading Nature's Signs: Use Outdoor Clues to Find Your Way, Predict the Weather, Locate Water, Track Animals—and Other Forgotten Skills*. New York: The Experiment, 2014.

Greer, John Michael, and Christopher Warnock, trans. *The Complete Picatrix: The Occult Classic of Astrological Magic—Liber Atratus Edition*. San Francisco: Adocentyn Press, 2010–11.

Goukassian, Elena. "Another Cat in the Wall." *Lapham's Quarterly*. November 26, 2019. https://www.laphamsquarterly.org/roundtable/another-cat-wall.

Grimassi, Raven. *The Witch's Familiar: Spiritual Partnerships for Successful Magic*. St. Paul, MN: Llewellyn Publications, 2003.

Harner, Michael. *The Way of the Shaman*. 10th Anniversary Edition. San Francisco: HarperOne, 1990.

Heinlein, Robert A. *Stranger in a Strange Land*. New York: Berkley Publishing, 1961.

Hoggard, Brian. *Magical House Protection: The Archaeology of Counter-Witchcraft*. New York: Berghahn Books, 2019.

Huson, Paul. *Mastering Witchcraft; A Practical Guide for Witches, Warlocks and Covens*. New York: Putnam, 1970.

Illes, Judika. *The Encyclopedia of Spirits: The Ultimate Guide to the Magic of Fairies, Genies, Demons, Ghosts, Gods & Goddesses*. New York: HarperCollins, 2009.

Johnston, Edward. "Witche Ways." In *The Witches' Almanac; Aries 1973–Pisces 1974*. Edited by Elizabeth Pepper and John Wilcock. New York: Grosset & Dunlap, 1973.

Kachuba, John B. *Shapeshifters: A History*. London: Reaktion Books, 2019.

Kelden. *The Crooked Path: An Introduction to Traditional Witchcraft*. Woodbury, MN: Llewellyn Worldwide, 2020.

King James. *The Annotated Daemonologie: A Critical Edition*. Edited by Brett R. Warren. Amazon Books, 2016. First published 1597.

———. *The Annotated Daemonologie: The Wonderful Discoverie of Witchcraft*. Amazon Books, 2019. First published 1619.

Laird, Tessa. *Bat*. London: Reaktion Books, 2018.

Leddy, Gabriela Garcia. "'One May be an Imp as well as Another:' The Familiar Spirit in Early Modern English Witchcraft Pamphlets." PhD thesis, University of York, 2017.

"Leviticus 20:27–King James Version." BibleGateway. Accessed December 31, 2023. https://www.biblegateway.com/passage/?search=Leviticus%2020%3A27&version=KJV.

Lupa. *Fang and Fur, Blood and Bone: A Primal Guide to Animal Magic*. First edition. Stafford, England: Megalithica Books, 2006.

———. *Skin Spirits: The Spiritual and Magical Uses of Animal Parts.* Stafford, England: Megalithica Books, 2009.

Matthews, John, and Caitlin Matthews. *British & Irish Mythology: An Encyclopedia of Myth & Legend.* London: Diamond Books, 1995.

Meyer, Regula. *Animal Messengers: An A–Z Guide to Signs and Omens in the Natural World.* Translated by Ariel Godwin. Rochester, VT: Bear & Company, 2002.

Myers, Arthur. *Communicating with Animals: The Spiritual Connection Between People and Animals.* Chicago: Contemporary Books, 1997.

"Newes from Scotland. Declaring the Damnable Life and Death of Doctor Fian a Notable Sorcerer, Who Was Burned at Edenbrough in Ianuarie Last. 1591." John Gray Centre. Accessed March 1, 2023. https://www.johngraycentre.org/wp-content/uploads/2021/11/Newes-From-Scotland.pdf. Originally printed for William Wright.

Nicols, Thomas. *Lapidary or, The History of Pretious Stones.* Cambridge, UK: Printed by Thomas Buck, 1652.

Potts, Thomas. *Discovery of Witches.* Project Gutenberg. Accessed May 22, 2023. https://gutenberg.org/cache/epub/18253/pg18253-images.html.

Pitcairn, Robert. *Ancient Criminal Trials of Scotland.* Vol. 3, part 2. Edinburg: 1833.

Patterson, Steve. *Cecil Williamson's Book of Witchcraft: A Grimoire of the Museum of Witchcraft.* London: Troy Books, 2014.

"Rainbow Bridge Poem." RainbowBridge. Accessed June 2023. https://www.rainbowsbridge.com/Poem.htm.

Reibetanz, John. "Sam Appleby, Horseman." *Poetry* 133, no. 4 (January 1979): 218–19. https://www.jstor.org/stable/20593311.

Sax, Boria. *The Mythical Zoo: Animals in Myth, Legend, and Literature.* New York: Overlook Duckworth, 2013.

Scott, Martin, and Gael Mariani. *Crystal Healing for Animals.* Moray, Scotland: Findhorn Press, 2002.

Serpell, James. "Guardian Spirits or Demonic Pets: The Concept of the Witch's Familiar in Early Modern England, 1530–1712." In *The Animal/Human*

Boundary: Historical Perspectives. Edited by Angela N. H. Creager and William Chester Jordan, 157–90. Rochester, NY: University of Rochester Press, 2002.

Seymour, John D. *Irish Witchcraft and Demonology.* London: Humphrey Milford, 1913.

Sheldon, Natasha. "'Thou Shalt Not Suffer a Cat to Live': Why Pope Gregory IX's Vox in Rama Implicated Cats in Devil Worship." History Collection. Accessed October 28, 2023. https://historycollection.com/thou-shalt-not-suffer-a-cat-to-live-why-pope-gregory-ixs-vox-in-rama-implicated-cats-in-devil-worship/.

Shipman, Pat. "The Animal Human Connection and Human Evolution." *Current Anthropology* 51, no. 4 (August 2010): 519–38. https://doi.org/10.1086/653816.

Simpson, Jacqueline, and Steve Roud. *A Dictionary of English Folklore.* Oxford: Oxford University Press, 2000.

Skelly, Joseph Paul. "Keep the Horseshoe Over the Door." In *The Ingalls Wilder Family Songbook.* Edited by Dale Cockrell. Published for the American Musicological Society. Middleton, WI: A-R Editions, 2011.

Smithsonian books in association with the National Museum of the American Indian, Smithsonian Institution. *Do All Indians Live in Tipis?: Questions and Answers from the National Museum of the American Indian.* Washington, DC: Smithsonian Institution, 2019.

Taylor, Thomas, trans. *The Hymns of Orpheus.* Philadelphia: University of Philadelphia Press, 1999. https://www.theoi.com/Text/OrphicHymns1.html #30.

von Uexküll, Jakob. *A Foray into the Worlds of Animals and Humans: With a Theory of Meaning.* Translated by Joseph D. O'Neill. Minneapolis: University of Minnesota Press, 2010.

Valiente, Doreen. *An ABC of Witchcraft Past & Present.* New York: St. Martin's Press, 1973.

Watson, Giles. *A Witch's Natural History.* First North American edition. Woodbury, MN: Llewellyn Publications, 2020.

"What Is CITES?" Convention on International Trade in Endangered Species of Wild Fauna and Flora. Accessed October 24, 2023. https://cites.org/eng /disc/what.php.

Wilby, Emma. *Cunning Folk and Familiar Spirits: Shamanistic Visionary Traditions in Early Modern British Witchcraft and Magic.* Eastbourne, England: Sussex Academic Press, 2013.

———. "The Witch's Familiar and the Fairy in Early Modern England and Scotland." *Folklore* 111, no. 2 (October 2000): 283–305. https://doi.org /10.1080/00155870020004648.

William, Shakespeare. *Macbeth.* Folger Shakespeare Library. Accessed October 28, 2023. https://www.folger.edu/explore/shakespeares-works/macbeth /read/4/1/.

Winter, Sarah Kate Istra. *Working with Animal Bones: A Practical and Spiritual Guide.* Self-published, 2014.

The Wonderful Discoverie of the Witchcrafts of Margaret and Phillip Flower, Daughters of Joan Flower neere Beuer castle: Executed at Lincolne, March 11.1618 Who were specially arraigned and condemned before Sir Henry Hobart, and Sir Edward Bromley, Judges of Assize, for confessing themselves actors in the destruction of Henry Lord Rosse, with their damnable practices against others the Children of the Right Honourable Francis Earle of Rutland. Together with the severall Examinations and Confessions of Anne Baker, Joan Willimot, and Ellen Greene. Witches in Leicestershire. London: G. Eld for I. Barnes, dwelling in the long Walke neere Christ-Church, 1619. Digital Witchcraft Collection. Accessed April 2, 2023.

Yong, Ed. *An Immense World: How Animal Senses Reveal the Hidden Realms Around Us.* New York: Random House, 2022.

To Write to the Author

If you wish to contact the author or would like more information about this book, please write to the author in care of Llewellyn Worldwide Ltd. and we will forward your request. Both the author and the publisher appreciate hearing from you and learning of your enjoyment of this book and how it has helped you. Llewellyn Worldwide Ltd. cannot guarantee that every letter written to the author can be answered, but all will be forwarded. Please write to:

Dodie Graham McKay
⁒ Llewellyn Worldwide
2143 Wooddale Drive
Woodbury, MN 55125-2989

Please enclose a self-addressed stamped envelope for reply,
or $1.00 to cover costs. If outside the U.S.A., enclose
an international postal reply coupon.

Many of Llewellyn's authors have websites with additional information and resources. For more information, please visit our website at http://www.llewellyn .com.